"With incisive precision, clarity, and refreshing veracity, Coppola's *Literacy for All* offers a framework that equips readers with the tools needed to engage in expansive literacy practices that underscore the cognitive and social aspects of literacy, support the internal and external work necessary to sustain liberatory literacy practices and honor the research and scholarship of those whose expertise, though critical, is often not centered. This work is a vital addition to your literacy instruction toolkit."

—Afrika Afeni Mills, Author of *Open Windows, Open Minds: Developing Antiracist, Pro-Human Students*, Education Consultant, Adjunct Instructor, and CEO of Continental Drift, LLC

"*Literacy for All: A Framework for Anti-Oppressive Teaching* walks readers through literacy movements and current debates while maintaining a critical lens on how our identities and relationships to communities impact our teaching. Coppola brings a wealth of knowledge about the definitions of literacy, sociocultural approaches to literacy, and ways to unmask the oppression embedded in dominant narratives of literacy instruction. This book carefully looks across literacy theory and methods through the lens of a thoughtful framework that recognizes the role of our positionalities, the internal and external work that is necessary when teaching, and the research-based approaches we must be aware of if we are indeed doing literacy work that is transformative and liberating. *Literacy for All* is a must-read for all teachers, literacy coaches, and those who want to nurture an anti-oppressive literacy culture in their schools. This book will impact our teacher journeys and help transform institutions."

—Carla España, Assistant Professor of Bilingual Education and Puerto Rican/Latinx and Latin American Studies, Department of Puerto Rican and Latino Studies, Brooklyn College, City University of New York

"*Literacy for All* is a call for a more focused, complete, and unflinchingly honest approach to building literacy. Coppola brings expertise, experience, and, most importantly, humanity to the national discussion around literacy education. Melding important research from many different realms of education and holding them all up equally for important findings and critical analysis, *Literacy for All* is a book that anyone involved in education will find helpful, meaningful, and thought provoking."

—Tom Rademacher, Author of *It Won't Be Easy* and *Raising Ollie*

"Wow! Shawna Coppola has created a comprehensive yet digestible literacy framework that envelops an enormous breadth of research and history without overwhelming readers. She lays out why we must enact classroom and systemic change but more importantly, she shows educators how. Yes, this is the path to *Literacy for All*. More aptly, even, Required Reading for All."

—Nawal Qarooni, Educator, Author, and Literacy Expert

*"Literacy for All* is an active book. In its pages, Coppola demonstrates the ongoing, alive, and continual excavation required to challenge our enculturated norms. More than a simple *how-to*, the book is a conversation that asks you to dig and then keep digging. Grounded in scholarship, while remaining utterly approachable, *Literacy for All* will help you peel back the layers of your instruction, question who is best being served, and challenge you to do better."

—Christopher Lehman, Founding Director,
The Educator Collaborative

# LITERACY FOR ALL

**An equity-conscious, culturally sustaining approach to literacy education.**

Every student comes to the classroom with unique funds of knowledge in addition to unique needs. How can teachers celebrate and draw upon the valuable literacies each child already possesses to engage them more effectively in school literacy practices?

In *Literacy for All*, Shawna Coppola shows how a literacy pedagogy founded on anti-oppressive principles can transform the experiences of teachers and students alike. Using her framework, which highlights the social and cultural aspects of literacy, teachers can help students participate in literacy experiences that illuminate their individual strengths.

Coppola's book, an ideal introduction for equity-conscious literacy educators, shows how to design instructional and assessment practices that reflect both the cognitive processes and the social practices inherent in learning to read and write.

**Shawna Coppola**, MA, a former classroom teacher and literacy specialist, is an active school consultant, a community leader, and a faculty member in the Learning Through Teaching program at the Literacy Institutes of the University of New Hampshire. She lives in Madbury, New Hampshire.

## Equity and Social Justice in Education Series
Paul C. Gorski, Series Editor

Routledge's Equity and Social Justice in Education series is a publishing home for books that apply critical and transformative equity and social justice theories to the work of on-the-ground educators. Books in the series describe meaningful solutions to the racism, white supremacy, economic injustice, sexism, heterosexism, transphobia, ableism, neoliberalism, and other oppressive conditions that pervade schools and school districts.

*Teaching Asian America in Elementary Classrooms*
Noreen Naseem Rodríguez, Sohyun An, and Esther June Kim

*Literacy for All: A Framework for Anti-Oppressive Teaching*
Shawna Coppola

*Social Studies for a Better World:*
*An Anti-Oppressive Approach for Elementary Educators*
Noreen Naseem Rodríguez and Katy Swalwell

*Equity-Centered Trauma-Informed Education*
Alex Shevrin Venet

*Learning and Teaching While White:*
*Antiracist Strategies for School Communities*
Jenna Chandler-Ward and Elizabeth Denevi

*Public School Equity: Educational Leadership for Justice*
Manya C. Whitaker

*Ableism in Education: Rethinking School Practices and Policies*
Gillian Parekh

# Literacy
## For All

### A Framework for
### Anti-Oppressive Teaching

## Shawna Coppola

Routledge
Taylor & Francis Group

NEW YORK AND LONDON

Designed cover image: © Getty Images

First published 2024
by Routledge
605 Third Avenue, New York, NY 10158

and by Routledge
4 Park Square, Milton Park, Abingdon, Oxon OX14 4RN

*Routledge is an imprint of the Taylor & Francis Group, an informa business*

ISBN: 978-1-032-59714-0 (pbk)
ISBN: 978-1-032-65896-4 (ebk)

DOI: 10.4324/9781032658964

Typeset in Garamond
by codeMantra

**Note to Readers:** Models and/or techniques described in this volume are illustrative or are included for general informational purposes only; neither the publisher nor the author(s) can guarantee the efficacy or appropriateness of any particular recommendation in every circumstance. As of press time, the URLs displayed in this book link or refer to existing sites. The publisher and author are not responsible for any content that appears on third-party websites.

For Maureen

# Contents

# Acknowledgments

I recently had the opportunity to spend an entire day in community with members, supporters, and leaders of a local antiracist organization as part of their volunteer-training program. Part of the day's work involved using the Building Movement Project's Social Change Ecosystem Map (2018), created by author and activist Deepa Iyer, on the individual roles we played within a larger ecosystem—in the dismantling of racial oppression.

With the support of our dynamic facilitator, Kevin, I was able to identify fairly quickly what roles I connected to most readily (*disruptor, weaver, guide*) as well as what roles I felt less connected to. In addition, I was able to identify the roles that others with whom I am in community around this work often play (e.g., *caregiver, storyteller, builder*). Kevin helped me and the rest of my co-conspirators to think deeply about *why* we connected to certain roles over others and how important it is to ensure that we are "in relation" with folks who help round out our ecosystem and hold us accountable to our goals around equity and justice.

In that spirit, I would like to thank the team at W. W. Norton as well as the following individuals with whom I am grateful to be in community and whose work/feedback/very existence has contributed enormously to the book you hold in your hands:

The *visionaries*, the *experimenters*, and the *disruptors*: Kate Lucas, Paul Gorski, Lorena Germán, Andrea Bien-Asciola, my colleagues at the Racial Unity Team, and students from whom I have had the utter privilege to both teach and learn over the years;

The *builders* and the *caregivers*: Janet N. Y. Zarchen, Kathy Collins, Kristin Forselius, Christopher Lehman, and all of the talented thinkers and doers at The Educator Collaborative;

The *storytellers* and the *healers*: Tomasen Carey, Dr. Towanda Harris, and Ijeoma Ogwuegbu (whose gorgeous, vibrant artwork I spent hours staring at in my office when my writing brain threatened to shut down in protest);

The *guides* and the *weavers*: Jennifer Borgioli Binis; Alex S. Venet; Christina Ortmeier-Hooper; my editor for this book, Carol Collins; and my forever editor and friend, Maureen Barbieri;

And finally, everlasting thanks to my absolute, most favorite *frontline responder* and life partner, David Coppola. You and our girls—including our tiniest, furriest one—are everything to me.

# Introduction

I am someone for whom literacy—*print* literacy, anyway—came both rapidly and easily. I have very early memories, made more vivid with photographs, of pretending to be "sick" so I could lounge on our '70s-era davenport in my footie pajamas and "read" my mom's magazines, of lying in bed with my dad at bedtime as he read every word—copyright page included!—of *The Runaway Bunny*.

I was accurately reciting *The Monster at the End of This Book: Starring Lovable, Furry Old Grover* by age 2, gleefully shouting out the names of street signs from the back seat of the car at 3. When I began reading my grammy's old, musty Nancy Drew books at age 4, I was declared "gifted" and promptly enrolled in a local, private kindergarten where, for the very first time in my life—

—I felt utterly and hopelessly inept.

Now, to be fair, my first kindergarten teachers had a bit of a cruel streak—or at least, it seemed that way to my 4-year-old self. I can remember, for example, how they'd lock the bathroom door after recess and force my classmates and me to wait until returning home to relieve ourselves, spanking us in full view of one another when we failed to properly control our biological needs. But beyond the day when I became the unlucky recipient of The Spanking, there is one other unsavory kindergarten memory that's seared into my brain: the time my teachers shamed me for failing to understand an assignment's directions.

You see, my early entry into schooling (and of being labeled as "gifted") was precipitated solely by my literacy life—specifically, my reading and writing practices. Here's the rub: I could successfully decode words (thanks, *Sesame Street*!) and had become quite adept at both writing my name and copying words that I was intrigued by. But like many children who lack sufficient background knowledge, I had zero clue what I was reading—or writing—the vast majority of the time. I was 4, remember; my life experiences as a White girl growing up in rural Maine didn't extend much beyond playing with Matchbox cars, rolling precariously down grassy hills, and watching *Bozo's Circus* every morning.

Thus, when the time came for me to actually apply my decoding and encoding skills to meaningful tasks, like deciphering the directions on a worksheet, I felt like one of the villains in *Scooby-Doo* during each episode's Great Unmasking: I was a fraud, a sham, an imposter. Most of the time, the activities my classmates and I were invited to do in our kindergarten spaces—cutting and pasting, learning to play leapfrog—were important (and fun!). And I excelled at a lot of them. This one task, however, was different—and Reader, I choked. I tried so hard to wrap my brain around what my teachers were directing us to do (something to do with mailing addresses? I still don't know), but my little 4-year-old brain just couldn't figure it out. In response, they pursed their lips and glared at me from behind their giant spectacles, convinced I was being purposefully defiant. I stared down at my worksheet and cried while some runny-nosed 5-year-old—most likely a Tommy or a Jason or a Kenneth—snickered at how "dumb" I was. (They were decidedly proficient at whipping out such ableist slurs at a moment's notice, those kids.) After what seemed like hours, one of my teachers heaved a giant sigh. "Go sit on the rug," she barked, her hands resting on her polyester-clad hips. "I'm calling your mother."

I share this story because, while my memory may be somewhat unreliable 42 years later (although I don't think so! Those teachers were downright *scary*), it illustrates the sheer lack of support I felt as a student of literacy in my first "official" classroom space. However, it's also important to acknowledge that this was one of very few utterly degrading moments I experienced throughout my K–12 schooling as a White, cisgender, able-bodied girl whose literacies and languages outside of school matched, with uncanny precision, the literacies and languages that were, and continue to be, privileged and taught in school spaces. Like a good number of my peers, I grew up in a home with an unending supply of books featuring characters who looked and talked like me; my lived experiences often reflected those of the fictional children I read about in mathematical word problems and on standardized tests. Heck, the very ways *I matched letters and sounds together* were—and still are— considered "universal" or "standard." You know how some parents ask children questions that they already know the answer to but pretend not to (e.g., *What should you be doing right now?*) instead of telling them directly to do something (e.g., *Get your shoes on, please*)? Even those specific discourse patterns— the ones I was accustomed to using at home—matched those that my own teachers engaged in. School—and school-based literacy— was, quite frankly, designed with children like me in mind. As we know all too well, this is entirely not the case for far too many children and youth—most often, Black, Brown, and Indigenous children and youth—whose rich and diverse literacies and languages often do *not* match those most valued in schools (Baker-Bell, 2020; Kinloch et al., 2017).

## WHAT EXACTLY IS "STANDARD" ENGLISH?

In his piece "Reading 'Whiteness' in English Studies," rhetoric and composition scholar Timothy Barnett (2000) argues that notions around "standard" English fail to illuminate what he calls the "white ground" (p. 10)—the ideological, if often invisible, positioning that considers White, middle-class ways of speaking and writing as superior to non-White ways of speaking and writing and that perpetuates White dominance in academic/educational spaces.

The idea of there being such a "standard," maintained both by academic elites and by K–12 practitioners, is a perfect example of the ways in which oppression "hides" in broad daylight when it comes to literacy practices, policies, and curricula—and its potential for enacting harm can begin early on in a child's school experience. For example, scholars of African American Vernacular English, or AAVE, have long identified some common phonological differences between speakers of AAVE and speakers of White Mainstream English* (Baker-Bell, 2020), including "r"-lessness, "l"-lessness, and the "simplification" of final consonants (such as when dropping or reducing the final "d" in the word "friend"). Unfortunately, many educators consider these phonological features to be deficits (i.e., *sub*standard), leading some Black children to be misidentified early on as in need of literacy intervention. (I circle back to this phenomenon in Chapter 4.) A good number of literacy assessments most commonly used to screen children for reading and writing difficulties perpetuate this practice, devoting only a few sentences in their scoring guides to warning educators about "penalizing" a student for "varied pronunciation due to consistent dialect, accent, or articulation differences" (University of Oregon, 2021, p. 49).

*In her book *Linguistic Justice: Black Language, Literacy, Identity, and Pedagogy*, Dr. April Baker-Bell (2020) uses this term in place of "Standard American English" in order to highlight the relationship between language, race, and racism.

## Why This Book? Why Me? Why Now?

If you're a critical consumer of professional books like the one you now hold in your hands, you may be thinking, "Why should I be turning to you—a self-described White, cisgender, able-bodied woman—to teach me about anti-oppressive literacy education? Why shouldn't I be reading Drs. Gholdy Muhammad, Liza Talusan, Kimberly Parker, and Felicia Rose Chavez?" To that I say, *you 100%, unequivocally should*. This book is not meant to supplant, undermine, or appropriate the work of these important author-educators, nor that of the work of scholars like Dr. Laura Jiménez and Jessica Lifshitz and Nawal Qarooni, who generously share their work and thinking about literacy and education frequently both on and off social media. Rather, this book is meant as a humble companion to the work of these scholars whose shoulders

I stand on; a curation of everything I have learned and, more importantly, *unlearned* about teaching literacy over the quarter century that I have spent as an educator and the almost half century (gulp!) I've spent as a human being in community with others.

This process has not been easy; no learning process is perfectly linear, and it's all the more true when we, particularly we White folks, have been socialized to be complicit in the oppression of others, whether it's due to the racial, social, political, or professional power we have (or have at particular times, in specific contexts). Fortunately, there are actions that we can take, *starting today*, to build the mindsets and habits necessary to help us collectively and consistently work toward developing an anti-oppressive practice. Not only will this book highlight some of the concrete actions we can take in order to make our literacy practices more inclusive and humanizing, it will offer the *why* behind them—the reasons why these practices are so essential—all of which is contextualized through a sociohistorical lens that helps us understand precisely how we got to where we are today.

In addition, as a middle-aged White woman in a profession teeming, statistically speaking, with middle-aged White women (Will, 2020), I feel a compelling obligation to, as the saying goes, "collect my people" and share what I have learned in order to help others learn as well. For many years, I was a card-carrying member of the "system is broken" crowd. (Sound familiar?) I would shake my head sadly, muttering at our country's "broken system" of education. It wasn't until I read Dr. Carol Anderson's book *White Rage: The Unspoken Truth of Our Nation's Divide* (2016) that I realized, mid-career, that the educational system was not *broken*, but rather was working *exactly as it was designed*—from its very inception. As I began to thread together the history of our education system and how literacy fits into this system, I realized with dawning horror the many specific ways in which I had been complicit not only in the continued oppression of children whose languages and literacies did not fit the dominant mold, but in the racist, classist, and ableist narrative that school-based literacies and language practices ought to be molded on White, middle-class, Eurocentric practices. *How could I have not seen this before?* I wondered.

## TO CAPITALIZE OR NOT TO CAPITALIZE?

You may or may not have noticed that, in this book, I am choosing to capitalize all races and racialized identities, including "White." While there is quite a robust debate around this practice, I have opted to capitalize both "White" and "Whiteness" when I am using these terms as racial and political concepts to signify their racial and political significance. (Shout-out to my colleague Lorena Germán for schooling me around this.) Too often, those of us who are White consider our Whiteness to be invisible or part of a "default" identity, whereas Black and Brown folks are situated as "other." I wish to disrupt this practice by using the capital "W."

This book is my attempt to help others "see"—see that the vast majority of literacy education in our nation's K–12 schools works not to liberate but largely, instead, to oppress those who don't fit the dominant, White, Eurocentric idea of what it means to be a reader, writer, and speaker. It is also designed to help educators consider the many ways in which we can proactively disrupt this oppressive system not only within our classrooms but within ourselves—particularly when done in community with, and accountability to, others. In doing so, though, I must acknowledge the tension around my taking on work like the writing of this book, which includes a constant negotiation around and assessment of when to "step up" and call in those who are also complicit in literacy-based oppression versus when to "pass the mic" so that the work of my colleagues who are disabled, transgender, and/or unprotected by the guise of Whiteness is heard and celebrated. After exploring the number of similarly themed professional books for literacy educators on the market and conferring with a number of colleagues, I made the decision to take this opportunity to model what this might look like as a White, cis, able-bodied woman with a specific, if limited, set of knowledges.

So the time, frankly, is now.

## MIND THE GAP

The term "achievement gap" was first coined alongside the publication of the 1966 Coleman Report (officially titled *Equality of Educational Opportunity*), which, among other things, examined the standardized test results of students of varying racial and ethnic identities and found a considerable difference between their performance on the tests—even while at the same time acknowledging that these assessments, and others like it, are not "culturally fair" and are in fact "[designed] . . . to determine the degree to which a child has assimilated a culture appropriate to modern life in the United States" (Coleman et al., 1966, p. 218).

Forty years later, Dr. Gloria Ladson-Billings (2006) implored educators, researchers, and policy makers to "call into question the wisdom of focusing on the achievement gap as a way of explaining and understanding the persistent inequality that exists (and has always existed) in our nation's schools," arguing that, in truth, what we have is not an *achievement* gap, but rather an "education debt." Other scholars, among them American sociologist Prudence L. Carter and education professor Kevin Welner (2013), have proposed the term "opportunity gap," pointing out that achievement and opportunity are "intricately connected. Without one, you cannot have the other." We will examine the "gap" concept more thoroughly in Chapter 1.

## How to Get the Most out of This Book

While this book will offer a variety of ways in which we might revise our practices as literacy educators in order to make them more inclusive and anti-oppressive, it's important to acknowledge that sustained change cannot happen in a vacuum. Schools reflect the communities that they serve, and a community that does not support—let alone work to implement—the kinds of large-scale changes that are necessary for disrupting dominant (e.g., White, patriarchal, cis-hetero,

Christian, able-bodied) norms is bound to obstruct or undermine any attempt at this kind of change within a school. For more on this, check out some of the research on successful school-community partnerships that I recommend.

## SCHOOL-COMMUNITY PARTNERSHIPS

There is a vast collection of research that demonstrates how important it is for schools and communities to work alongside each other to increase positive outcomes for all, particularly when it comes to issues around equity and access. While Chapter 4 offers some guidance for getting to know our students' families, the following texts are also among those that I have found most helpful to understanding how to create effective school-community partnerships that avoid perpetuating existing power dynamics:

"From Positivism to Critical Theory: School-Community Relations Toward Community Equity Literacy" by Terrance L. Green (2017)

"Beyond Involvement and Engagement: The Role of the Family in School–Community Partnerships" by Amanda Stefanski, Linda Valli, and Reuben Jacobson (2016)

"Fostering Educational Resilience and Opportunities in Urban Schools Through Equity-Focused School–Family–Community Partnerships" by Julia Bryan, Joseph M. Williams, and Dana Griffin (2020)

"Strong School–Community Partnerships in Inclusive Schools Are 'Part of the Fabric of the School. . . . We Count on Them'" by Judith M. S. Gross, Shana J. Haines, Cokethea Hill, Grace L. Francis, Martha Blue-Banning, and Ann P. Turnbull (2015)

"Meeting, Knowing, and Affirming Spanish-Speaking Immigrant Families Through Successful Culturally Responsive Family Engagement" by María L. Gabriel, Kevin C. Roxas, and Kent Becker (2017)

In addition, because I am a White woman educator who has largely worked in predominantly White schools and communities, it is essential to read this book in partnership with works (books, articles, social media posts, etc.) written by educators whose identities and lived experiences differ from my own. I have taken great care to amplify and cite the work of many of these folks throughout these pages. That said, it will be important to read Chapter 1, in which I lay out my anti-oppressive literacy education framework and its guiding principles, before diving into any of the other chapters. The succeeding chapters (Chapters 2–6) more deeply explore each of the guiding principles of the framework and are arranged in a way that makes it easy to "dip in and out" of those that you find the most novel or interesting and read them in the order you choose. However, I must emphasize that these principles overlap and are not meant to be studied or embodied in isolation, but as part of a comprehensive educational praxis. As part of that praxis, each chapter will offer some suggestions for engaging in "internal" as well as "external" work that you might take on as someone committed to anti-oppressive literacy education. *Please do not skip or gloss over the internal work!* Doing so will prevent us, as a collective, from building the capacity necessary to sustain this work over the long term and to transfer the insights we've gained through engaging in such work to diverse situations and environments. And build capacity we must!

> To my Black, Brown, Indigenous, and AAPI colleagues: Some of my "internal work" suggestions might cause you discomfort. While some level of discomfort is okay (and even useful for growth), please be mindful of when the discomfort veers into a place that feels harmful and shift your focus to caring for yourself.

Finally, a caveat: engaging in anti-oppressive work is 100% best done in community with others who have shared goals. It can often be tough, to say the least, to find allies and co-conspirators who are willing—and able—to take the risks necessary to disrupt dominant norms and practices. If possible, try to find folks to explore this text with, whether it be in person or virtually, and commit to holding one another (and me, too!) in loving accountability to the kind of literacy practices and mind shifts that, ultimately, will serve the readers and writers with whom we work in the ways that they truly deserve.

## ACCOUNTABILITY & ALLYSHIP

In her essay "Developing a Liberatory Consciousness," consultant, author, and lecturer Dr. Barbara J. Love (2013) writes about the four elements necessary to being an effective liberation advocate which are "meant to serve as reminders in our daily living that the development and practice of a liberatory consciousness is neither mysterious nor difficult, static nor fixed, or something that some people have and others do not" (p. 600). These elements are *awareness*, or living life "from a waking position," which allows us to take notice when oppression occurs; *analysis*, which builds upon these noticings, seeks to understand them, and determines what ought to be done to disrupt them; *action*, or speaking up when oppression occurs and organizing around shared anti-oppressive goals; and *accountability/allyship*, which involves a commitment to working in community and collaboration with others who are invested in disrupting and dismantling oppression. Dr. Love writes, "Accepting accountability to self and community for the consequences of actions taken or not taken can be an elusive concept for a people steeped in the ideology of individualism," but that we must "always question, explore, and interrogate ourselves about possibilities for supporting the efforts of others to come to grips with our conditioning into oppression, and give each other a hand in moving outside of our assigned [social] roles" (p. 603).

## Internal Work

- Consider your own literacy history. What experiences do you remember from your childhood/youth (both inside and outside of school)? How might this have shaped your notions about what it means to be "literate"?
- In this introduction, I've offered some insight into some of my own varied and complex identities. What are yours? How would you describe your race, ethnicity, gender, first language? Are you able-bodied or disabled? Neurotypical or neurodivergent? What is your immigration status? Reflect on how you think these identities shape you as both a learner and an educator. (*You can read more about identity and how it relates to power and oppression in Chapter 3.*)
- Were your K–12 school literacy experiences designed with someone like you in mind? How do you know? If not, how do you wish things had been different?

## External Work

- List three to five students you have (or have had) who you consider to be "successful" readers and/or writers. What qualities or practices make them "successful" in your mind? Then, list three to five students you consider to be "struggling" or "reluctant" readers or writers. Jot the practices or behaviors they engage in that cause you to include them in this list. What do you notice about the two lists? What patterns do you see? What do you wonder about them?
- More list-making! Think about who you are already in community with (or who you might *want to be* in community with) around this work. Together, begin to brainstorm a plan for action. How will you engage in this work together? How often will you meet to check in and discuss what's going well or what's not going well? In what ways will you hold yourself accountable to one another (and to your students)?

# LITERACY FOR ALL

# CHAPTER 1

# The Anti-Oppressive Literacy Education Framework

*The act of learning to read and write . . . is a creative act that involves a critical comprehension of reality.*
—Paulo Freire and Donaldo Macedo (1987), *Literacy: Reading the Word and the World*

In this chapter, I plan to introduce the anti-oppressive literacy education framework that I've developed with you all. But first, I want to share a story of how what some perceive to be "good intentions"— something most educators have an abundance of!—can inadvertently cause harm.

In September of 2012, I was working as a literacy specialist and coach in a small K–6 school in rural New Hampshire. Although I could do without the lunch duties and the endless meetings and the dozens of trips to the microwave to reheat my long-suffering cup of morning coffee, I loved my job. I loved my colleagues, who graciously invited me to co-plan and co-teach with them as much as our busy schedules would allow. I loved my principal, who truly understood how messy and nonlinear and beautiful learning could be. Most of all, I loved my students, who were constantly surprising me with their noticings and their wonderings and the ways in which they taught me what it meant to be a reader and a writer.

That same month, Irene Fountas and Gay Su Pinnell, creators of the F&P Text Level Gradient and two of the leading voices in reading instruction, put out a white paper through their publisher that explained

DOI: 10.4324/9781032658964-1

their decision to make "minor adjustments" (2012a, p. 1) to the grade-level reading goals on their gradient, which had long been a ubiquitous tool used in schools across the country. These adjustments—minor though they appeared on paper, and despite the authors' warnings to educators about using the new gradient to identify more children as being "at-risk" as readers—ultimately increased the literacy expectations of children in kindergarten and Grade 1 due to what the authors perceived as evidence that young children's literacy development was increasing at a rapid rate. In their white paper, they pointed to the fact that children were living in a world "substantially different" from that of a decade prior; that preschools were more frequently incorporating literacy into their play-based programs; and that "many children" were now entering kindergarten "with a strong foundation of knowledge surrounding literacy" (p. 1). In addition, they cited numerous studies that demonstrated "a steady trend upward" (p. 2) in the literacy skills of children who'd previously been enrolled in full-day kindergarten, which matched their own on-site observations, interviews, and data collection.

## THE F&P TEXT LEVEL GRADIENT

The F&P Text Level Gradient™ is a tool designed by Irene Fountas and Gay Su Pinnell that was originally intended to be used by classroom teachers and other literacy professionals in selecting books to use for small-group reading instruction. However, in practice, it is most often used in conjunction with their Text Level Ladder of Progress (2012b) as a guide to determine where students should "be" as readers at the end of a particular grade level. Despite the authors' consistent suggestions that educators adjust their expectations of students as readers "based on school/district requirements and professional teacher judgment" (2012a, p. 2), too often it is used as a tool to label children as "in need of intervention" if they do not reach the suggested grade-level goals at various points throughout the school year. You can read more about this tool and its intended uses at https://www.fountasandpinnell.com/textlevelgradient/

As a result of all of this, the authors wrote (2012a), "recommended entry-, mid-, and exit-level [reading] goals, as well as intervention goals, must change" (p. 2). The revised F&P Text Level Gradient™

- offered clearer delineations between grade-level expectations,
- removed all overlaps between grades
- included higher text-level expectations for readers at the end of kindergarten and Grade 1

Let's set aside, for now, that the idea of a child reading "on level *x*" is in itself a fallacious concept due to variations in their background knowledge, first language, and interests. (the authors themselves had previously conceded this in their book *Guiding Readers and Writers (Grades 3-6): Teaching Comprehension, Genre, and Content Literacy*, stating that "individual students cannot be categorized as, for example, 'level M readers'" [Fountas & Pinnell, 2001, p. 225]). According to the revised gradient, a student in Grade 1 reading at a Level C in October—previously considered to be "on track" with their peers—would, under the guidelines of the new gradient, suddenly appear to be severely below grade level and in dire need of reading intervention.

This consequence of the revised tool was alarming in itself, and my colleagues and I, after much deliberation, opted to reject it—something Fountas and Pinnell are *clear to note* is an acceptable choice—in an attempt to resist what we considered to be yet another unfair increase in literacy demands for children. (Around this time, the Common Core State Standards had just been released, and we were pretty salty about the accompanying push for ever-greater "text complexity" across the grades as well, which—again—served to increase the number of students who were thereafter identified as "in need of intervention.")

## The Importance of Paying Attention to Research—and to How It's Interpreted

Equally alarming, however, and something I did not fully realize until several years after first reading their 2012 white paper, was that some of the studies that the authors cited—and used to make their revisions to the gradient—were troublesome. For example, one study they cited (Votruba-Drzal et al., 2008) revealed the following deficit-laden belief, couched as fact, in an attempt to argue the benefits of full-day kindergarten: "Children from economically disadvantaged households *tend to experience less consistent, supportive, and cognitively stimulating caregiving* than those from middle- and upper-class families" (p. 958; emphasis added). In my view, knowing that the researchers behind this study hold such beliefs—enough to state them explicitly in this paper—renders the research itself problematic.

If the research itself was not problematic, the revision to Fountas and Pinnell's Text Level Gradient based on *their interpretation of the research* was. In another study they cite in their white paper (Ackerman et al., 2005), the researchers note that the academic/literacy benefits of attending full-day kindergarten "seem to be greater for disadvantaged children" (p. 11). But the increased reading expectations that would result from accepting and implementing the revised gradient would, in effect, mean that those same children would perceptually lose any literacy "advantage" they had potentially gained from attending full-day kindergarten. If more educators had paid attention to these citations— and how they were ultimately used to guide the revision of the F&P's Text Level Gradient™—would there have been greater resistance to the revised tool and its accompanying increase in expectations of student readers? Would we have anticipated the influx of deficit-minded ideas around how many students were now, suddenly, "in need" of intervention? Perhaps; perhaps not.

All of this is not to pick on Drs. Fountas and Pinnell, whose work I greatly respect and who have contributed an enormous amount to the field of literacy education. (While I focus on this particular example here, you will see, as you move through this book, that I am an equal-opportunity critic—including of my own practice as an educator. Rather, my intention is to illustrate the often unintended— but nevertheless real—harm that can result from failing to use an anti-oppressive framework to enact literacy practices, policies, and curricula. Sadly, this is but one of an overwhelming number of examples I could have used to illustrate how resulting policies or changes in practice, even those that are well-intended, can contribute to the oppression of our most vulnerable students. Our profession—nay, our country's very *history*—is full of them.

---

### DEFINING OPPRESSION

Founded in 1987 by a group of progressive philanthropists dedicated to supporting equity and justice efforts, the Chinook Fund (https://chinookfund.org) uses the generally accepted definition of oppression, which conceptualizes it as being the result of prejudice plus power. However, they have gone a step further in order to identify *four specific types of oppression* (Chinook Fund, n.d.):

* *ideological oppression* (based upon a dominant group's *ideas* about another group);
* *institutional oppression* (that which is embedded in societal institutions like education, health care, and the legal system);
* *interpersonal oppression* (e.g., the kinds of prejudicial mistreatment that happen between individuals or groups of people); and
* *internalized oppression* (when members of an oppressed group come to believe that they're deserving of discrimination or disrespect due to their own inherent failures).
* Playwright and actor Eliana Pipes, in collaboration with the Western Justice Center, created a short video explaining each of these four types of oppression called *Legos and the Four I's of Oppression* that's 100% worth checking out (https://youtu.be/3WWyVRo4Uas).

---

## "Gap" Language and the History It Obscures

Take the omnipresent narrative of America's literacy "achievement gap." While the "gap" terminology was not coined—or propagated by the media—until the mid-1960s (see my introduction for a brief history around this), the hard truth is that we have *always* witnessed a "gap" in the ways in which literacy has been in/accessible to those living on this land. For example, in the decades leading up to the Civil War, many Southern states made it outright illegal to teach enslaved Africans to read or write for any reason other than to promote "Bible literacy." The main purpose of this one allowance was to maintain religious devotion to White, Christian values. Teaching or promoting what historians called "liberating literacy" (Clifford, 1984; Cornelius, 1983)—i.e., literacy that promoted an individual's social mobility and/or contributed to a diversity of thought—to those who were enslaved was punishable by steep fines (if the person was considered White) and physical punishment or jail if the person was not (e.g., was a free Black person). Even in states where schooling for free Black children existed—for example, in Massachusetts, New York, and Pennsylvania—"suspicion and surveillance of black education prevailed" (Givens, 2021, p. 11).

Once the Civil War ended and Reconstruction was underway, the number of schools established for the education of both White and Black children exploded, and the "gap" persisted in areas of the United States where the literacy education of Black children was systematically disrupted. In some cases, this disruption was perpetrated by White property owners who refused to lease their land for the purpose of building schools that would educate African American children (Scribner, 2020); in other cases, White folks attempted to destroy schools entirely (such as in Virginia, where "Black schools and churches used for educational activities were routinely burned" [Givens, 2021, p. 32]).

## DISRUPTING, DISMANTLING, AND DREAMING

Despite the ways in which gatekeepers of literacy in the United States have built systems and created policies that oppress communities of individuals unprotected by Whiteness, these communities and individuals have engaged in powerful campaigns throughout history that actively resist these efforts—even (and often) when their very lives were/are at stake. For example, despite slave codes throughout the antebellum South prohibiting the teaching of enslaved folks to read and write

English, thousands of enslaved individuals nevertheless acquired English print literacy through subversive means, such as teaching what they'd learned from being in proximity to their masters and mistresses during the day to other family members at night under the cloak of darkness (Cornelius, 1983).

Post-Emancipation, under the tyranny of Jim Crow, many African Americans created literary societies for themselves "when access to formal institutions was denied or when the opportunities in formal institutions [e.g., American schools] was substandard" (Fisher, 2004). In the late 1960s, student activists who were part of the Chicano movement fought for the right to speak their native language, Spanish, in school spaces. And in 2017, seven student plaintiffs in Detroit, Michigan, sued then-governor Rick Snyder over deplorable school conditions that they claimed violated their right to a "basic minimum education," which includes the opportunity to learn to read and write at a "functional" level (*Gary B. v. Snyder*).*

*You can read more about how literacy has historically been used as a tool of oppression, and how marginalized communities have fought against these efforts, in Chapter 6.

This "gap," of course, was perpetuated not just among Black children but among Indigenous children as well. In the mid-17th century, beginning with the establishment of the Virginia legislature's plan to "bring them up in Christianity, civility, and the knowledge of necessary trades" (Bremner, 1970, p. 4), Indigenous children were kidnapped from their families and forced to suppress their Native literacies and languages in order to assimilate to White, Eurocentric notions of what it meant to be "literate." While both Chinese and Japanese children were systematically excluded from public schools in California throughout the 19th and early 20th centuries, Japanese-language schools in Hawaii and California were specifically targeted by U.S. legislators concerned by a fear of "anti-American sentiment" (Douglas, 2015). And during the mid-20th century, segregated Latinx and Hispanic students often had only the secondhand books they could scrape up from neighboring White schools to read and were paddled or otherwise punished for speaking their native language on school grounds (Hennessy-Fiske, 2022; Ruiz, 2001).

## WHITENESS

It is important to keep in mind that the protection of Whiteness, or what critical race theorist and legal scholar Dr. Cheryl I. Harris (1993) calls "the set of assumptions, privileges, and benefits that accompany the status of being white" in America (p. 1713), has not always been conferred onto those with light skin and other external physical characteristics. For example, certain heritage classes or ethnic groups who emigrated to America in the early 20th century who are *now* considered to be White (e.g., Irish, Italians) were not initially offered the protection of Whiteness. In addition, while the U.S. Census Bureau currently defines "White" as "a person having origins in any of the original peoples of Europe, the Middle East, or North Africa" (https://www.census .gov), many members or descendants of these populations, particularly within the latter two regions, are often not awarded the societal privileges associated with Whiteness.

Two resources that I have found useful in developing my own understanding around the fluidity and complexity of Whiteness—and of race in general—are the three-part video series *Race: The Power of an Illusion* (Pounder et al., 2003) and *Seeing White* (Biewen, 2015), a 14-part documentary podcast from Scene on Radio and the Center for Documentary Studies at Duke University.

I could, of course, go on. The truth of the matter is that the literacy "gap" that we have witnessed play out over time in the "achievement" scores of White children versus those who do not benefit from Whiteness is nothing new and cannot possibly be understood without understanding how our dominant literacy educational practices, both in school and out, are *designed to uphold this gap*. Please understand, however: This is not to equate, say, the burning of schools that educated Black children during Reconstruction with the revising of a popular tool used to assess readers and/or the accessibility of print text. My goal here is only to point out that there is an inherently oppressive thread that connects these actions together over the course of a long and complex history. And while embracing an anti-oppressive literacy education framework will not itself repair all of the historical harm done to students or create a more just, equitable world, it is surely a step in the right direction.

## THE "LITERACY MYTH"

Coined in 1979 by the social historian and professor of English at Ohio State University Harvey J. Graff, the "literacy myth" refers to the exorbitant power attributed to literacy that diminishes (or, in some cases, outright ignores) the effects that social and structural inequalities based on race, ethnicity, class, and other attributes have on the lives of individuals. In his 2010 essay "The Literacy Myth: Literacy, Education and Demography," Graff writes that "part of what makes . . . assumptions about the benefits of literacy a myth is that they are not universally true" (p. 18), although he concedes that the development of dominant forms of literacy *does* often play a part in individuals' ability to attain social, economic, and political capital (e.g., through occupations that rely on print literacy). I highlight his work here to emphasize that the embracing and enacting of the anti-oppressive literacy framework that I lay out in this book is not meant to be a panacea for all of education's (or society's) ills, and must be enacted *in conjunction with* other policies and practices that work toward creating a more just and equitable world for all.

## The Anti-Oppressive Literacy Education Framework

The framework (Figure 1.2) for enacting anti-oppressive literacy practices, policies, and curricula that I have developed and will elaborate on throughout this book arose out of the key values and principles I've identified as essential to embodying this kind of work. And I want to be 100% honest: Over the almost 25 years that I have been an educator, I have engaged in many, many practices and policies and used or designed a number of curricula that have decidedly *not* been anti-oppressive in nature. I am not perfect, nor do I believe that I—or anyone else, for that matter—will ever be entirely "anti-oppressive." I am a member of numerous communities and institutions, both literal and metaphorical, that were built in a way that ensures the maintenance of White, cis-hetero, patriarchal, able-bodied privilege and power. I have also been socialized to maintain this power and privilege, which means I have a lifetime of learning and unlearning to do. For example, after a number of years of identity and resistance work in both my personal and professional life, I still sometimes default to a sexist, racist, and/or ableist mindset, particularly during times of stress or fatigue. This can show up in the ways I initially react when someone calls me out—or in—for a harm I have caused or when I make assumptions about, say, what types of literacy practices a student and their family engages in at home. However, I am committed to using every resource at my (often privileged) disposal to engage in this important work, and part of that is encouraging my colleagues to both *internalize* and *seek to educate others around* the following five key principles.

As you explore the framework, please note how the key principles and values I've included are not mutually exclusive, but instead overlap with one another to form a comprehensive mindset. In addition, please approach this framework as a dynamic one that will likely be further developed and refined over time in order to reflect new—and deeper—understandings.

# THE ANTI-OPPRESSIVE LITERACY EDUCATION FRAMEWORK *

**LITERACY INVOLVES BOTH COGNITIVE PROCESSES AND SOCIAL PRACTICES**

Literacy practices–even those that involve a unique set of cognitive requirements–are socially, culturally, and historically situated (Li, 2001; Muhammad, 2020; Street, 2001). As such, they reflect both the worldviews and the ideological assumptions of those who engage in such practices.

**IDENTITY AND LITERACY ARE INEXPLICABLY LINKED**

Our social identities, ideologies, and lived experiences all influence the ways in which we think about, and engage in practices around, literacy. Texts by themselves do not hold meaning; rather, it is through the interaction, or "transaction," between the reader and the text (Rosenblatt, 1978), that meaning is made visible.

**ALL HUMAN BEINGS ENGAGE IN LITERACY & LANGUAGE PRACTICES THAT ARE BOTH VALID AND VALUABLE**

Despite what so many have been socialized to believe, and what we are implicitly taught in the majority of school spaces, there is no one universal way to be literate; each of us is "highly literate in at least one ... context" (Carter, 2006).

**MEANING-MAKING OCCURS WITHIN A VARIETY OF EQUALLY VALID COMMUNICATIVE CHANNELS OR MODES**

While alphabetic text has traditionally been most privileged in the vast majority of school spaces (Coppola, 2019), understanding how to "read" and compose visual, aural, and other modes of text is equally important, and equally valuable, in today's world.

**LITERACY CAN BE USED AS A TOOL FOR LIBERATION AS WELL AS A TOOL FOR OPPRESSION**

Power shapes literacy practices, influencing notions around who is deemed "literate" and who is not, as well as whose stories are (and have historically been) deemed worthy of expression, exploration, and study vs. whose are not.

Coppola, 2022

*Educators who embody an anti-oppressive educational literacy practice both recognize and seek to educate others around these key principles.*

**Figure 1.1**   The Anti-Oppressive Literacy Education Framework

## Principle #1: Literacy involves both cognitive processes and social practices.

Literacy—and its attendant practices—is neither neutral nor apolitical. Part of why this is true is because, as many scholars have demonstrated, literacy practices are socially, culturally, and historically situated (Heath, 1982; Li, 2001; Muhammad, 2020; Street, 1984). As such, they reflect both the worldviews and the ideological assumptions of every person who engages in literacy practices. When we say that literacy is socially situated, we mean that despite prevailing ideologies, there is no single literacy practice—or set of practices—that can be decontextualized from the kinds of power structures that play out in society. What, how, when, and with whom we read, write, and speak is all tied up in how we are positioned, and how we position ourselves, within larger contexts and communities.

### THE CYCLE OF SOCIALIZATION

Social justice educator Bobbie Harro (2013) developed her "Cycle of Socialization" in order to represent how the process of socialization begins, how it affects our lives, how it's perpetuated by systems and institutions, and what happens when we disrupt the cycle in an attempt to create change. At the core of the cycle are the forces that often keep us *in* the cycle: fear, ignorance, power, and so forth. For example, before my students taught me the many ways that they make meaning beyond reading or writing exclusively print text, my ignorance kept me from questioning the overprivileging of print text in schools and classrooms (even despite what I was experiencing, and had experienced, through my own literacy practices; see more about this in Chapter 5).

Surrounding this core are the many ways in which our unquestioned beliefs and practices are both developed and maintained: through people we know and trust, through the media, through institutions such as schooling and health care, and so forth. As Harro writes, "Those who stay in line [with our socialized beliefs and practices] are sanctioned, while those who don't are punished, persecuted, stigmatized, or victimized" (p. 46). The result of these enforcements is that the cycle perpetuates itself, maintaining inequities, misconceptions, and even, for those with less power, internalized oppression: "We live with or promote the status quo; we choose not to make waves; we do nothing, and the cycle continues."

For example, the fact that I am able to write and publish this very book you hold in your hands is connected to the power I have within the profession, which is itself connected to my dominant social identities. I have (somehow) built a reputation of being a knowledgeable, somewhat affable literacy practitioner who rarely misses an opportunity to point out why a practice is inequitable or why a text is problematic. The very fact that I feel comfortable doing this—despite the ways in which it has gotten me in hot water more than a few times throughout my career!—speaks to the social, professional, and even financial capital that I benefit from. And the fact that this reputation has gained me professional opportunities like the writing and publishing of this book must be acknowledged.

Alongside all of this resides the fact that print literacy—literacy that relies on the accurate decoding, encoding, and comprehending of written symbols and texts for communicative purposes (Purcell-Gates et al., 2004)—involves a particular set of cognitive requirements within each individual in order to establish proficiency. When we hear practitioners as well as non-educators referring to the "science of reading" (SoR), for example, this is typically what they are referencing: the need to teach individuals how to "crack the code" of letter-sound relationships *while also* teaching them how to comprehend written language. However, the vast body of research from which the SoR community draws, as well as the individuals conducting said research, cannot be separated from, or remain untouched by, social, cultural, and political contexts and forces. For example, many of the most oft-cited scholars (Linnea C. Ehri, Phillip P. Gough, William E. Tunmer, Keith E. Stanovich, Louisa Moats,

Stanislas Dehaene, etc.) who conduct research around how individuals learn to read have come from WEIRD (Western, educated, industrialized, rich, and democratic) societies (Heinrich et al., 2010) and are overwhelmingly White. In addition, when conducting research around the "science" of reading, most, if not all, of these scholars are conducting research around how individuals learn to read English or similar alphabetic texts; this, despite the fact that the majority of the world's population "learn[s] to read and write in non-European, nonalphabetic orthographies" (Share, 2021, p. S391) such as Inuktituk, Arabic, and Japanese. Thus, it is important to understand all literacy practices as being influenced by and as influencing *both* social and cognitive forces.

When referencing the "science of reading" or the "SoR" in these pages, I am generally referencing the common discourse or movement that is most often reflected in the media and not the more comprehensive "sciences" of reading that include research conducted within the fields of sociolinguistics, cultural anthropology, rhetoric studies, and so on. I do so because it is the movement, alongside the powerful dyslexia lobby, that has had the greatest impact on both state and district literacy policies as of late.

## Principle #2: Identity and literacy are inextricably linked.

Connected to the previous principle, our positionality—including our social identities, our ideologies, and the lived experiences that shape our position relative to power—influences the ways in which we think about, and engage in practices around, literacy. As I wrote in the introduction to this book, the fact that my languages and literacies very seamlessly matched the languages and literacies that I was exposed to and taught about in school spaces had an enormous influence on how I engaged in literacy practices throughout my K–12 experience. Not only that, but I grew up in a family where *everyone* read: books, magazines, catalogs, comics, cereal boxes, you name it. I never wanted for reading material, even if it came from the 10-cent table at the neighborhood yard sale, nor was I prohibited from reading anything I happened to find. (Hello, V. C. Andrews and Stephen King!) I also spent a lot of time engaged in literacy-rich play at my grandparents' and friends' houses throughout my childhood; because each of these spaces was safe and secure, and because I always had enough food to eat and enough seasonally appropriate clothes to wear, I was rarely asked to help out with more than light chores or to watch my younger siblings and, instead, had enormous privilege and freedom to play card and board games, explore an inordinate number of (overflowing) bookshelves, and sing or dance to my heart's content.

In addition, as I mentioned previously, I almost always saw myself represented in the books that I read and that were read to me; as a result, I was highly motivated to read and had the confidence to stick with print texts that were somewhat challenging. For better or worse, my teachers and family members identified me very early on as a "writer," too, which caused me to also self-identify as a writer. (I was convinced I was going to be the next Erma Bombeck or Dave Barry.) And while I devoured comics as a child, it wasn't until several years ago, when an explosion of graphic novelists and webcomic creators who identified as women came onto the scene, that I convinced myself to try my own hand at creating comics, which I dabbled in quite a bit for a hot minute. In short: Identity matters—in these ways and more—when it comes to our literacy practices, both in and out of the classroom.

### Principle #3: All human beings engage in literacy and language practices that are both valid and valuable.

Here are some statistics for you:

- According to the 2019 edition of The Nation's Report Card (Conroy, 2021), 82% of Black fourth graders, compared to 66% of all fourth graders, were determined to be reading at a level below "proficiency." 0% were assessed to be reading at an "advanced" level.
- Black children are less likely to be identified with dyslexia when compared to their White peers. At the same time, they are more likely to be referred to special education (Conroy, 2021).

- American Indian/Alaska Native students are 1.8 times more likely, and Hispanic or Latinx students 1.1 times more likely, to receive special education services for a specific learning disability compared to all other racial/ethnic groups combined (Office of Special Education Programs, 2007).
- Students who are identified as emergent bilinguals (commonly referred to as "English Language Learners" or "ESL [English as a Second Language] students") are disproportionately represented as having a specific learning disability or as being in need of "intervention" (Linan-Thompson, 2010).

What "story" do these education statistics tell? Some would (mistakenly) point to this data as evidence that many children from these particular racial, ethnic, and/or linguistic groups lack the foundational skills, including the foundational literacy skills, necessary to achieve "grade-level performance" in school. That it is imperative that they receive the "intervention" they need, as early as possible, to help them "catch up" to their more affluent, and/or monolingual peers (Goodrich et al., 2017; Kelly et al., 2008). This narrative is a misrepresentation of one of many underlying issues.

One of the most important underlying issues is in how we define literacy, and what it means to be literate. While there are, of course, students who truly do need accommodations and/or a modified curriculum to help them realize their full potential as learners within the system we currently have, it is also important to understand that, despite what many of us have been socialized to believe, there is no one universal way to be literate—or to use language. As Shannon Carter (2006), associate professor of English at Texas A&M University, writes in her piece "Redefining Literacy as a Social Practice," "we are all highly literate in at least one . . . context" (p. 100), regardless of whether these contexts mirror those that have historically been most valued in school spaces. Anti-oppressive literacy educators spend less time and effort on attempting to "fix" their students or on bemoaning their performance on assessments that privilege dominant literacy practices and more on using their own pedagogical expertise, alongside their professional and social capital, to nurture a learning environment that recognizes, values, and builds upon the literacy and language practices that their students *already have.*

## Principle #4: Meaning-making occurs within a variety of equally valid communicative channels or modes.

While alphabetic text has traditionally been most privileged in the vast majority of school spaces (Coppola, 2019), understanding how to "read" and compose visual, aural, and other modes of text are equally important in today's world. Whenever I am working with a group of literacy teachers around this, I ask them to think about the last four to five units they've taught or themes of study they've engaged in with students. Then we consider some of the most common reading and writing practices that children and youth engage in outside of school spaces, which often include scrolling through and/or posting on their social media, creating TikToks, and so forth. We examine these lists to see if they match up with one another—and of course they don't. Yet despite the ubiquity of multimodal literacy practices in *most of our* lives—not just in the lives of youth—we continue to make instructional and curricular choices in school that send the message that these practices are less important, or worse—subpar.

> Not for nothing, education and literacy experts have been saying this same thing for years; for example, one of my favorite quotes comes from the 1969 book *Teaching as a Subversive Activity*, in which the authors, Neil Postman and Charles Weingartner, write that "certainly printed media and the printed book in particular will continue to exert powerful influences on society. . . . But equally certain is the fact that print no longer 'monopolizes man's symbolic environment,' to use David Riesman's phrase" (p. 165).

This is particularly harmful for students whose culturally informed literacy practices include telling stories and sharing histories through the use of a wide variety of media and materials (as through Indigenous beading practices) or modes (e.g., spoken word poetry). In addition, our collective overprivileging of primarily alphabetic texts—whether we are reading or writing them, or inviting our students to read or write them—continues to marginalize those whose strengths and talents become more readily apparent with the inclusion of opportunities to read and to write multimodal texts. Does this mean that every literacy educator should immediately take up collage or, say, podcasting? Not necessarily. However, incorporating a wider variety of media, modes, and forms in our literacy practice is much more inclusive of a diversity of cultures, languages, interests, and lived experiences.

### Principle #5: Literacy can be used as a tool for liberation as well as a tool for oppression.

Power shapes literacy practices, influencing notions around who is deemed "literate" and who is not, as well as whose stories are deemed worthy of expression, exploration, and study versus whose are not. When educators and other individuals in positions of power implicitly or explicitly marginalize or outright dismiss the literacies of those whose practices differ from dominant notions of literacy, they enact harm.

Furthermore, throughout history, individuals and groups who have traditionally maintained political, social, and economic power in the United States have used a variety of gatekeeping practices to determine *who is* and *who is not* granted access to literacies of power—that is, those literacies that privilege White, Eurocentric ways of reading, writing, and speaking. Therefore, as critical literacy scholar Hilary Janks (2010) reminds us, "how we teach literacy can make a significant difference to the ways in which the cultural and linguistic capital, associated with powerful discourses, dominant languages, elite varieties and elite literacies, are distributed" (p. 133). This is especially crucial to consider when the demographics of the education profession within the United States continue to favor those who, like me, have a relatively large amount of social, cultural, and linguistic privilege compared to that of much of our student population, whose racial, ethnic, and linguistic identities continue to shift and diversify (National Center for Education Statistics, 2021).

Friendly yet firm reminder that, *regardless* of our student population, continuing to develop an anti-oppressive literacy pedagogy is essential for working toward the collective liberation of everyone—*including* those who hold dominant identities and who have been socialized to uphold White supremacist systems and institutions.

## Before Proceeding . . .

Based on your own theoretical ancestry, you may be more familiar with some of the key values and principles that make up this framework than with others. If that's the case, it will be important for you and your colleagues to spend time discussing the principles with which you are, in a thereotical sense, less familiar and perhaps diving more deeply into some of the scholarship surrounding them before moving on to the succeeding chapters. Without an acceptance of these ideas firmly in place, it will be challenging to honestly consider the questions I will be posing at the end of each chapter and effectively put into practice the suggestions I will be making in each of them. Having said that, let me be clear that the suggestions I make are not part of a comprehensive list that's meant to be taken or used as a step-by-step procedure (and, considering my identities and lived experiences, may not make sense for you or the students with whom you work). As I mentioned earlier, becoming an anti-oppressive literacy educator is not a destination, but a lifelong journey—for me included!—and *you* may know your students and what their particular needs might be better than I do.

### Internal Work
- Think about how you have been socialized, both in and out of school spaces. Which of the key values and principles from the anti-oppressive literacy education (AOLitEd) framework are you *most* challenged by, due to this socialization? In other words,

which one(s) do you have the hardest time embracing, and why? Which AOLitEd principles are you least challenged by?

- What narratives around the literacy "achievement gap" have you been exposed to in your own schooling or professional practice? When have you and your colleagues been complicit in perpetuating this narrative? After having learned some history around it in this chapter and in the introduction, do you feel any different about it than you did before, or was your own thinking around it affirmed by this history?

## External Work

- Work alongside your colleagues to create a table like the one I have designed (Table 1.1) that considers where literacy oppression currently "lives" in your school. Keep this table handy as you progress through the chapters of this book. As you read, ask yourselves: Within our district/school/classrooms, what are some of the literacy policies, practices, and/or curricula that may contribute to the oppression of students based on one or more of their social identities? Whose identities are *centered* in these policies, practices, and curricula? Whose are not? What proposed revisions or solutions might we—and might we invite our students to—consider?

- In addition, or perhaps in place of the previous suggestion, use the AOLitEd Framework Worksheet I have designed (see appendix) to jot your thinking—as well as your noticings and wonders about your own educational space(s) and practices—as you move through each chapter. This is also a good place to document any critical feedback or questions you have *for me*, which I am always happy to hear. (You can contact me via my website, https://shawnacoppola.com)

**Table 1.1:** Where Does Literacy Oppression "Live" in Our School?

| Policy/Practice/Program (or aspect of school culture) | Whose Literacy Practices Are Centered? | Whose Are Not? | Solutions/ Proposed Revisions |
|---|---|---|---|
| [EXAMPLE] Centering of White stories & voices in literature & other texts in literacy curricula | White folks, Euro-American | Black, Brown, Indigenous, AAPI voices/perspectives | Supplant or supplement these texts with those that offer more windows, mirrors, & sliding glass doors (Bishop, 1990) alongside #OwnVoices authors (Duyvis, 2015) |
| | | | |
| | | | |
| | | | |

| Policy/Practice/Program (or aspect of school culture) | Whose Literacy Practices Are Centered? | Whose Are Not? | Solutions/ Proposed Revisions |
|---|---|---|---|
|  |  |  |  |
|  |  |  |  |
|  |  |  |  |
|  |  |  |  |
|  |  |  |  |
|  |  |  |  |

# CHAPTER 2

# Literacy Involves Both Cognitive Processes and Social Practices

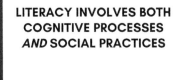

**LITERACY INVOLVES BOTH COGNITIVE PROCESSES *AND* SOCIAL PRACTICES**

Literacy practices–even those that involve a unique set of cognitive requirements–are **socially, culturally, and historically situated** (Li, 2001; Muhammad, 2020; Street, 2001). As such, they reflect both **the worldviews** and **the ideological assumptions** of those who engage in such practices.

*Literacy cannot be judged apart from some understanding of the social circumstances and specific historical traditions which affect the way this ability takes root in a society.*
    —Jenny Cook-Gumperz (1986), "Literacy and Schooling: An Unchanging Equation?"

DOI: 10.4324/9781032658964-2

When you think about the so-called Reading Wars, what do you think of? Most people consider there to be two distinct camps in this centuries-long battle about how best to teach children and youth to become "literate." The general perception is that in one camp are the "science of reading," or SoR, folks: those who embrace an ideology that posits that the way individuals learn to read is a "settled science"—that the decades of research within the fields of cognitive neuropsychology and developmental psychology prove that all children should be explicitly and systematically taught the same five components of reading; i.e., phonemic awareness, phonics, fluency, vocabulary, and comprehension (Stewart, 2020). While proponents of SoR sometimes allude to developmental differences in the ways that children might (or might not) benefit from the systematic, explicit teaching of the "Big Five," what the dominant science of reading narrative fails to do is grapple with any discussion of the social and cultural factors that affect the development of print literacy.

## THE READING WARS: A LONG HISTORY

It may surprise you to learn that arguments over how "best" to teach children to read and write have existed since—well, almost since children have been formally taught to read and write in American common schools. In the mid-19th century, after visiting a Boston school in which he observed students being taught to read using the alphabetic principle, and a German school in which students were taught to read using whole language methods, education reformer Horace Mann used his political influence to advocate for the latter method, which he saw as a more "kindly" way of teaching reading (Meltzer, 2020). Nearly 80 years later, the authors of *Elementary Principles of Education*, Edward L. Thorndike and Arthur I. Gates, declared that "artificial" classroom drills, like phonics drills, were "wasteful" and offered "intrinsically . . . little value" to students (Rochester, 2002). This was also around the time when Dr. Samuel Orton (of the famed Orton-Gillingham method) began to document what he considered the danger of popular contemporary methods of teaching children to read in a paper titled "The 'Sight Reading' Method of Teaching Reading, as a Source of Reading Disability," which was published in 1929 in the *Journal of Educational Psychology*.

In recent years, the so-called Reading Wars have taken on a more fervent tone as the media has perpetuated simplistic notions around what folks on each "side" of the battle believe (e.g., that SoR advocates promote a "phonics only" approach—untrue—while "balanced literacy" advocates promote a pedagogy that sneers at the inclusion of phonics instruction—also untrue). Unfortunately, this inaccurate and superficial narrative often dismisses important aspects of the discourse around how best to teach children to read and write that take into account sociocultural, political, and historical factors, such as those that I have tried to address in this book.

In the other camp are folks—generally characterized as proponents of "whole reading" or "balanced literacy"—many of whom believe that the ways in which individuals learn to read (and incidentally, to write) are greatly influenced by social, cultural, historical, and political factors and that, while teaching children the "Big Five" is important, such components do not constitute the "be all, end all" of literacy instruction. In addition, folks in the latter camp tend to resist legislative and other mandated efforts, born from SoR ideology and advocacy, that (if not in theory, in practice) require classroom teachers to teach the "essential skills" of reading in the same explicit, systematic way to the majority of students via "SoR approved" programs—often leading to the marginalization or exclusion of other important aspects of literacy instruction.

The messy truth is, both camps make valid points, and the (imagined) Venn diagram representing these camps overlaps in important ways. For example, there is, indeed, a body of research from the fields of cognitive psychology and neuroscience that demonstrates a number of what we currently recognize as empirical truths, the implications of which absolutely ought to be aligned with our literacy instructional practices. (I say "currently" because consensus within these communities is destined to change over time as we learn more about the nature of the human brain.) One is that our brains, while "hard-wired" to learn language, are not, at the present moment, hard-wired to learn to read print, which largely involves making connections between graphemes and spoken language. Another truth, as demonstrated by studies using functional magnetic resonance imaging, or fMRI, is that neurotypical brain processes involved in reading a word versus speaking a word appear to be different.

A grapheme is a written symbol, such as a letter or set of letters, that represents a sound. For example, the letter "c" can make the sound /k/ or /s/. The letter "x" can make the sound /ks/, or if at the beginning of a word (e.g., "xylophone"), /z/.

For example, when *speaking* a word, brain activity is detected as beginning along the middle of the left side of the brain and traveling downward and forward. Alternatively, when *reading* a word, brain activity appears to begin in the back of the brain—where much of our visual processing takes place—and spreads along the bottom surface and into the middle (Brem et al., 2010; Dehaene, 2011; Marinkovic et al., 2003). (Note that this is the case *at the word level only*; a 2019 study by postdoctoral neuroscience researcher Fatma Deniz and her colleagues at the University of California, Berkeley, found that when individuals listen to stories versus read them, brain imaging indicates that the activity involved in processing the meaning of the stories is almost identical.)

Such research indicates that, for neurotypical individuals whose first language shares a similar kind of orthography as English, learning to read (and write) printed words involves a cognitive process that is, indeed, universal; that doing so consists of "in the head" operations that, largely, are the same. This intellectual stance, and the assumptions that go along with it, aligns with what Brian Street, professor of language, education, and anthropology and one of the leading literacy theorists within the field, calls the "autonomous" model of literacy.

> Individuals who are categorized as dyslexic—estimations range any-where from 5% to 20% of the population—use a less-efficient "in the head" operation that involves an overreliance on working memory (Shaywitz, 2007).

## The Autonomous Model of Literacy

In an autonomous model of literacy, according to Street, literacy acquisition is assumed to involve solely internal or "in the head" operations and, as such, is an *apolitical, context-neutral*, skills-based process of learning to read and to write. However, as he pointed out numerous times throughout his life and career, such conceptualizations of what it means to be "literate," regardless of where or how the actual processes of learning to read or write take place, are highly reflective of dominant, Western notions of what it means to be a "proficient" reader and writer and, thus, are susceptible to oppressive practices. In his 2011 piece "Literacy Inequalities in Theory and Practice: The Power to Name and Define," he writes, "The assumption that literacy [is] in itself, autonomously, defined *independently of cultural context and meaning*, will have effects, creating inequality for those who 'lack' it and advantages for those who gain it . . . [and] is deeply ideological" (p. 581; my emphasis).

In other words, while a specific learning process, such as learning to read and write words, can reasonably be demonstrated as one that happens internally—that is, in the brain—it still cannot be decontextualized from social, cultural, historical, and political factors. The reason for this, as Street and others have pointed out, is because as human beings, we do not live or learn in a vacuum or a laboratory, but rather as members of a society within varying communities of practice.

This becomes clearer when we consider how someone—I, for example—engages with a text that reflects a community of which I am not myself a member. Let's say the text, excerpted from the Marinkovic et al. piece I cited earlier, is this one:

> *The spatiotemporal characteristics of the responses to spoken words observed in our study concur with other evidence. The earliest response was estimated to lie in the superior temporal area bilaterally at 55 ms after stimulus onset (Figure 1) and then spread to the auditory "belt" in the perisylvian region as reflected in N100m. Subsequently, activity spread along the auditory "ventral" stream into anterior and lateral areas of the STG, concurring with the analogy to the visual pattern recognition or "what" stream (Binder et al., 1997; Rauschecker and Tian, 2000). (pp. 5–6)*

I can, with a reasonable amount of accuracy, *decode* the words in this text, as I imagine most of you can. In the spirit of full transparency, though, I must admit how challenging it is for me to *comprehend* the string of words that I've decoded, even when accounting for the one word with which I am entirely unfamiliar ("perisylvian"). Surely my comprehension does not hinge on knowing what that one word means! What it does hinge on, rather, is both my background knowledge *and* my familiarity with this particular community and its ideological characteristics—its ideas, beliefs, languages, and accepted literacy practices. And because I have relatively little background knowledge about the human brain, and do not currently belong to a community of neuroscientists who write complex articles for medical journals (with their particular jargon and syntactical devices), I am not in the practice of reading—decoding *and* comprehending—these sorts of texts.

Most advocates of the SoR approach to teaching would agree that background knowledge is an enormous factor in individuals' learning to read—that this is evident in their embracing of Hollis Scarborough's "rope model" of reading (2001), which incorporates both "word recognition" and "language comprehension" skills (and which is reliant, among other things, on an individual's background knowledge). However, the notion that the acquisition of background knowledge is an apolitical or culturally neutral endeavor, implied in the absence of any discussion of sociocultural contexts and the emphasis on "settled science" in the popular SoR discourse, is troublesome.

> While there is a movement-within-the-SoR-movement to place more emphasis on developing students' background knowledge as part of comprehension instruction (that, unfortunately, persists in perpetuating "gap" discourse; e.g., Wexler, 2022), it still fails to account for the diversity of children's varying social and cultural knowledges and, instead, advocates for the teaching of so-called "core" concepts. One popular curriculum guide, for example, lists as part of the "core knowledge" for grade K the "voyage of Columbus in 1492" (Core Knowledge Foundation, 2010)—and it's exactly as problematic as you might imagine.

Let's think about how my experience of needing a *specific kind* of background knowledge to read the above passage relates to the literacy experiences of a good number of children, particularly Black, Brown, and Indigenous children, in typical U.S. public school spaces. While school spaces can be considered their own unique "communities of practice," the vast majority of sanctioned school literacy practices and norms generally reflect those of White, English-speaking, middle-to-upper-class communities. This positions many of those whose identities or practices do *not* reflect this demographic at a distinct disadvantage. For example, studies have shown that even the ways in which we ask questions in school and on standardized assessments—referred to in the literature as "known-answer questions"—frequently echo the questioning style of many White, middle-class, Euro-American caregiving adults, giving the children who come from these homes an advantage when it comes time for them to begin formal schooling (Delpit, 1988; Mehan, 1979; Rogoff et al., 2018). For scholars of Critical Race Theory, this advantage amounts to a kind of intellectual "property"—a "reward," in a sense, for conforming to "perceived 'white norms'" (Ladson-Billings & Tate, 1995, p. 59). James Collins, an American linguist who has studied the historical development of conceptions of literacy in both England and the United States, has described how the particular development of what educators would consider "schooled literacy" (Cook-Gumperz, 1986) —largely, those literacy practices that conform to White, English-speaking norms—"has slowly become *the* norm for all literacy . . . turn[ing] a prior diversity of literate practices into a stratified literacy" that is often considered to be "universalistic" and "context-independent" (Collins, 1989, p. 12).

## KNOWN-ANSWER QUESTIONS

Known-answer (or known-information) questions are those often used in school discourse, where the individual asking the question already has the answer—or at least, has an idea of what an appropriate answer would be. For example, a third-grade teacher asking her class, "Where do we keep the book-checkout log again?" is using an example of a known-answer question.

In her essay "The Silenced Dialogue: Power and Pedagogy in Educating Other People's Children," Dr. Lisa Delpit (1988) explicitly discusses the differences many ethnographic researchers have found that often exist among members of differing socioeconomic and/or racial groups in the ways that they interact with children verbally. For example, a working-class parent might direct their child to bathe at home by saying something like, "It's time for your bath," whereas a middle- or upper-class parent might ask, "Isn't it time for your bath?" When students are in a school or classroom where the latter, more "veiled," directives/comments are used, this can place some children—most often, Black and/or working-class children—at a disadvantage. Delpit argues that

*such veiled commands are commands nonetheless, representing true power, and with true consequences for disobedience. [But] if [they] are ignored, the child will be labeled a behavior problem and possibly officially classified as behavior disordered. In other words, the attempt by the teacher to reduce an exhibition of power by expressing herself in indirect terms may remove the very explicitness that the child needs to understand the rules of the new classroom culture. (p. 289)*

While it is important to always keep in mind that people who exist within the same social groups are not monolithic, I do think such research provides us with some interesting and important food for thought.

In her book *Linguistic Justice: Black Language, Literacy, Identity, and Pedagogy*, literacy and race scholar Dr. April Baker-Bell (2020) echoes this sentiment: "The ubiquity of whiteness in schools erroneously positions White Mainstream English-speaking students as academically prepared to achieve because their cultural ways of being, their language, their literacies, their histories, their values, and their knowledges are privileged in classrooms" (p. 20). This "positioning" of racially and culturally dominant ways of speaking, knowing, and engaging in literacy practices in school spaces, defined as "apolitical" or the "norm" within an autonomous model of literacy, can have real, lasting, and harmful consequences for those whose practices may fall outside of the accepted "norm."

## The Ideological Model of Literacy

In contrast to an autonomous model of literacy, an ideological model of literacy considers literacy to be not simply a series of discrete skills to be independently acquired—for example, a cognitive process by which the brain learns to decode and encode print text—but a dynamic, and historically and culturally situated, set of social practices. Practitioners who embrace an ideological model recognize the assumptions inherent in what "counts" as literacy (as well as in who is deemed to be "literate") and "seek to make explicit such underlying conceptions and assumptions" (Street, 2011, p. 581).

For example, an educator who embodies an ideological model of literacy may accept, for the time being, the ways in which cognitive neuroscientists have demonstrated how the neurotypical brain functions when speaking a word versus reading one. However, they would question both how an individual's cultural/community literacy practices also play a role in the process of learning to read and what kind of biases and assumptions the researchers conducting these kinds of studies possess. For instance, in the Marinkovic et al. study cited earlier—within which, by the way, the researchers failed to disclose their own social identities/positionalities—the study subjects were composed of nine right-handed men who were native English speakers and who were determined to have "no hearing or other neurological impairments" (p. 8). Would the researchers' study elicit the same results if any of the male subjects identified as part of a community that suffered centuries of ancestral trauma? What if they identified as "native" English speakers, but were also bi- or multilingual? I ask these questions not to imply that there may be inherent *biological* differences in how these subjects responded to the tasks in the study, but because how their brains responded to the tasks may have differed depending on the literacy practices of the communities with which these subjects identified.

In short, while it has been established by decades of research that there are internal, cognitive processes involved in learning to read and write, it is important for educators to *also* recognize and acknowledge—and teach their students to recognize and acknowledge—the influence of social and cultural practices on these processes; that "cognition [occurs] always within cultural contexts" (Purcell-Gates et al., 2004).

## Why Is This Important?

When literacy practices are situated as occurring both "in the brain" *and* within cultural, social, and political contexts, we are better able to both recognize and understand how the literacy practices of dominant communities are privileged in the vast majority of K–12 school spaces. This can help us acknowledge how these dominant literacy practices impact

| **Table 2.1:** Autonomous vs. Ideological Models of Literacy | |
| --- | --- |
| Autonomous models . . . | Ideological models . . . |
| • consider "literacy" to be apolitical or "neutral" (but are in fact located within Western, academic ideologies)<br><br>• locate literacy within the individual, decontextualized from their membership in social and cultural communities<br><br>• conceive of "literacy" as something that is (or can be) universally "acquired" using instructional practices that are "science"- or "research"-based<br><br>• often point to the literacy "achievement gap" as a justification for the focus on universal instructional practices<br><br>• tend to focus on print literacy "skills"—i.e., the decoding, encoding, and deciphering of print text<br><br>• hold political power in the form of practices and policies at world, national, state, and local levels<br><br>• are about teaching reading & writing | • conceive of literacy as a set of culturally defined, and thus political, "practices"<br><br>• locate literacy within both individuals who engage in literacy practices as part of social and cultural communities, *and* within these communities themselves<br><br>• consider many "research"- or "science"-based literacy instructional practices (and assessments) to be too narrowly focused on the decoding/encoding and deciphering of print text<br><br>• aim to contextualize and historicize ideas like the literacy "achievement gap" (or the ubiquitous literacy "crisis", as conceptualized by mainstream educational media)<br><br>• conceptualize "literacy" as something that includes orality as well as the reading and composing of visual, spatial, gestural, and multimodal "texts"<br><br>• are about teaching readers & writers |

- *what* literacy practices are taught;
- *how* literacy practices are taught;
- *how* these practices are assessed, evaluated, and reported; and
- *who* is ultimately identified as a "reader" or a "writer."

Such acknowledgment can also help us recognize and understand that, conversely, the social and cultural literacy practices of those who are not members of dominant (White, Euro-American, English-speaking) communities are often marginalized, disregarded, or dismissed, perpetuating deficit models and inviting both disengagement and, in some instances, psychological trauma.

## How We Teach Story Structure

Let's consider, for example, how children in K–12 classrooms (including, for many years, my own) are taught about "story structure." Most of the time, students are taught that the most effective narrative storytelling follows a structure developed in the 19th century by German playwright/novelist Gustav Freytag, called "Freytag's Pyramid." Within this structure, the exposition (setting and characters) of a story is established, alongside the story's central conflict, and proceeds to build toward the climax of the story through its "rising action." At or about the middle of the story occurs the climax; this is when, if composing a dramatic story, things begin to "fall apart" for the protagonist. (I used to teach my students that the climax didn't have to consist of one event but might consist of a series of important events that contain the most "energy" within the story.) The remainder of the story consists of the "falling action," where the tension from the main conflict begins to wane, eventually leading to the story's conclusion.

While a great many stories do follow this narrative structure—think of popular films like *The Hunger Games* or any number of stories within the Marvel Cinematic Universe—not all stories do. And yet so often, this is the only narrative structure that is taught in the vast majority of ELA classrooms. How many of us were taught a diversity of narrative structures situated in a wide range of cultural and social communities, such as the Robleto structure, which is based on traditional Nicaraguan storytelling, or story structures that reflect the oral traditions of Korea (*p'ansori*), Morocco (*hikayat*), or urban Black communities (e.g., toasting)?

## Dominant Practices Around Teaching Writing

Further examples of how most educators in K–12 spaces favor autonomous models of literacy—models that, again, favor "universal," context-"neutral," skills-based concepts of literacy—abound. For instance, let's think even more broadly about how writing is typically taught and assessed. While there are certainly classrooms in which students are invited to collaborate and to share their compositions, ideas, and processes, far too many employ practices that tell the "story" that writing is an internal, independent endeavor. In her book *ReWRITING the Basics: Literacy Learning in Children's Cultures*, researcher, author, and professor of education Anne Haas Dyson (2013) writes about how writing curricula, and consequently pedagogies, send the message that "to learn to compose, one goes inside oneself, applies oneself, does one's work; one does not play around with one's seatmates." She goes on to write, "There may be structured times when children are to share their plans with one another or provide editorial critiques to a partner. But often, the ultimate goal is for the individual to quite literally produce texts" (p. 6).

This tracks with my own experience as a student up through and including graduate school, where we were encouraged—or more often, required—to individually pump out text upon text upon text and rarely invited to collaborate on a composition (save for the occasional "group project"). It also, unfortunately, reflects much of my practice as a language arts teacher for the first decade or so.

Dyson also criticizes workshop approaches that teach young writers, in particular, to rely more on internal ideas—ideas about what to write about (from their own "real" experiences)—and less, if at all, on ideas they glean from their classmates and/or their worlds outside of school. However, as she and others (Cruz, 2015; Hagood et al., 2010; Newkirk, 2009) have pointed out, even these "internal" ideas are often subject to dismissal in the ELA classroom, particularly when they connect to topics within popular culture and *especially* when engaged in by boys and/or youth of color.

The devaluing and outright dismissal of pop culture within many literacy classrooms is ironic, considering that there is historical evidence to show that it was people's interest in engaging in popular culture (e.g., in participating in recreational activities like reading books, informally engaging in civic life, etc.) that spurred the development of a "commonplace literacy," and not economic necessity or widespread formal schooling, as is often assumed (Cook-Gumperz, 1986).

In "Cultivating Digital and Popular Literacies as Empowering and Emancipatory Acts Among Urban Youth," literacy and race scholars Marcelle Haddix and Yolanda Sealey-Ruiz (2012) point out that the social literacies that many Black and Brown boys engage in, which often include the uses of digital tools and popular culture, are frequently "pushed aside" or marginalized in favor of focusing on "official" school literacy practices. They wonder how the centering of dominant literacy practices, which frequently do *not* encourage the use of digital tools or popular culture, serves to control Black and Brown students and maintain power. Haddix writes,

> *We know that certain pedagogical and curricular practices can . . . leverage students' interests and choices in the topics, the genres, and the mediums and tools [students of color] use when composing in school. When we refuse to use and encourage such practices, I believe that this is intentional—we do not really want to close this so-called achievement gap. (p. 190)*

If we truly want to create school literacy spaces that are anti-oppressive, then we must begin by designing instructional and assessment practices that reflect *both* the cognitive processes *and* the social/cultural practices inherent in learning to read and to write.

## Acknowledging Both the Cognitive and the Social in Our Literacy Instructional Practices

One of the ways that we can do this is by designing literacy tasks that are authentic to children's lives outside of school spaces. I especially appreciate how literacy researchers Victoria Purcell-Gates, Erik Jacobson, and Sophie Degener (2004) define "authenticity" when it comes to literacy practices. For these scholars, the authenticity of literacy tasks exists on a continuum. On one side of the continuum are those practices that one might witness folks engaging in in the world outside of school: reading, writing, talking about, and listening to books, magazines, comics, social media posts, signs, food labels, song lyrics, and so forth. These are considered the *most authentic* kinds of literacy practices. On the other side of the continuum are those practices that would be considered the *least authentic* because they are considered "school-only" practices: completing worksheets, writing spelling or vocabulary lists, reading decodable texts, or responding to questions following the reading of a story or informational text.

### Task Authenticity

However, as Purcell-Gates and her colleagues point out, it's not just the specific practices that make a literacy task authentic or inauthentic, but the purposes behind these practices. For example, reading a novel may be considered more "authentic" than reading from a basal text, but its authenticity is decreased if the purpose of reading a novel is that it's part of the required reading list for a particular grade level, class, or team. Likewise, choosing an image and writing an Instagram caption may be considered an "authentic" task, but doing so as part of a class assignment from the perspective of a person from history (e.g., gay- and transgender-liberation activist Marsha P. Johnson) would make that task more school based.

This is not to say that every literacy task one invites their students to engage in needs to be 100% authentic; however, I do mean to suggest that we become (1) more knowledgeable about the kinds of literacy practices our students authentically engage in outside of school and (2) more mindful about incorporating some of these practices into our curriculum, instruction, and assessment.

For example, instead of assigning students to write book reviews, perhaps we might design an inquiry into the many ways that people use different practices for the purpose of recommending certain books to others or for sharing their love for particular books. In the world outside of school, these might take the form of

- creating whole-class, small-group, or individual recommended book lists to be distributed in bookstores or libraries;
- making book-recommendation cards that can be displayed underneath or inside a front-facing book;
- writing book reviews on a website like Goodreads or Amazon;
- creating a book-recommendation vlog post;
- creating a #BookTok post (using the TikTok app);
- starting a Twitter thread that tracks all of one's book recommendations for a period of time (e.g., a year or semester); or
- starting a #Bookstagram (using the Instagram app).

Spending time diving into what these practices have in common, and how they differ, can set the stage for students to make decisions about what book-recommendation practice would make the most sense for them.

Not only is increasing the authenticity of school-based literacy tasks essential to honoring both the cognitive processes and the social practices of literacy learners; it's more culturally responsive, as well. Compare, for example, prevailing African American ideas around learning—particularly literacy learning—around which there is much scholarship (Fisher, 2004; Muhammad, 2020; Winn, 2015; to name a few). In his chapter titled "'Knowledge Is Power': The Black Struggle for Literacy," historian Thomas C. Holt (1990) writes of the "preexisting cultural values" apparent among individuals in the newly freed African American community post–Civil War, particularly those who fought for a state-supported system of public education:

> *Traditionally and historically, for black Americans education has . . . served a profound social purpose; its goal is social, as well as personal, improvement—to uplift the people, to make conditions better. . . .*

*[E]ducation [is] the key to social change; it emanates outward from the individual to the larger group—to families and communities and eventually to the nation. (pp. 92–93)*

Throughout the decades, this "emanating" outward of knowledge—particularly through writing and orality—manifested in the establishment of Black literary societies (beginning in the early to mid-1800s), the Harlem Renaissance (1920s), the Black Arts Movement (1960s/1970s), Freedom Summer (1964), Black Twitter, and so on. In these (physical and digital) spaces, the purposes of literacy are deeply relational, and are reflected in practices that "spread the wealth" of knowledge among community members through discussion, informational texts (such as newsletters and pamphlets), art, or spoken word/song lyrics. (I return to this concept of "collective" literacy in Chapter 6.)

## WHAT DOES IT MEAN TO BE "CULTURALLY RESPONSIVE"?

The concept of culturally responsive teaching was first proposed by author, researcher, and professor of education Dr. Geneva Gay and itself builds upon the research and teaching of Dr. Gloria Ladson-Billings (1995), whose "culturally relevant pedagogy" rests upon the tenets of academic success, cultural competence, and critical consciousness. Dr. Gay's culturally responsive teaching (CRT) model honors the theoretical underpinnings of Dr. Ladson-Billings's work and moves even further to explicitly acknowledge and center the identities and lived experiences of racially and ethnically diverse learners.

CRT was theorized in response to the fact that too many U.S. educators, the majority of whom are White, are "inadequately prepared to teach ethnically diverse students" (Gay, 2002). It is grounded in the assumption that when school-based knowledge and skills are "situated" within these learners' identities, perspectives, and lived experiences, teaching and learning become more engaging, more effective, and more meaningful.

In addition to increasing the authenticity of the kinds of literacy practices we engage in alongside our students, it's important to make explicit the distinctions between "authentic" and "schooled" literacies to our students so that they can continue to develop their critical consciousness around literacy, its attendant practices, and systems of power. When we leave these kinds of distinctions "unsaid," or invisible, we fail to acknowledge the ways in which most school-based literacy practices reflect the particular institution that is schooling itself, along with the ways that they privilege certain kinds of practices over others. Such transparency is inherent and essential to teaching students to develop what Maisha T. Winn and Nadia Behizadeh (2011) call "hybrid literacy practices"—practices that "include multiple literate forms necessary for students and teachers to achieve critical literacies" and that allow students to both (1) access and engage in literacy practices of power (such as those most often assessed on high-stakes standardized tests) *and* (2) challenge narrow definitions of literacy "that perpetuate the discourse of deficiency" (pp. 151, 166).

## Independent Versus Collaborative Literacy Invitations

Another way that we can acknowledge both the cognitive and the social processes involved in literacy work is to aim for a better balance between practices that students engage in individually or independently and those they engage in collaboratively. For example, I have worked or volunteered in a number of schools that have implemented a "Book Buddy" program, where older students are paired with younger students in the same school or district and meet weekly to read with each other. This is advantageous to both groups of students, who are given an authentic social purpose for choosing an appropriate (i.e., interesting) book to read during their Book Buddy time as well as an authentic purpose for practicing important reading skills like prosody, expression, reading with accuracy, and talking about reading. In addition, this is a great way to build community within one's school or district while at the same time teaching students essential verbal and social skills that will serve them well in their lives both in and outside of school.

Many literacy educators, like authors Lisa Eickholdt and Patty Vitale-Reilly (2022), also advocate for the use of writing clubs, where students are grouped—or are invited to form their own groups—for the purpose of collaborating as writers. My own colleagues Kitri Schaefer and Lindsay Lanzer taught me the effectiveness of using writing clubs to help their fifth- and sixth-grade students who were writing in the same genre or form (e.g., comics, short stories) to (1) consider what made these distinct from other writing genres and forms, and (2) support one another during the process of composing. At other times, students participated in self-selected, temporary (2- to 4-week) writing groups based upon their perceived strengths (e.g., editing for clarity); classmates could at any time seek out the expertise of these groups in order to help them through a particular challenge during writing workshop time.

This imagining of literacy practices as a collaborative pursuit is not only potentially more engaging for a good number of students; it also acknowledges the reality that there are few literacy practices that are entirely solitary in nature. Phyllis M. Belt-Beyan says it best in her book *The Emergence of African American Literary Traditions: Family and Community Efforts in the Nineteenth Century* (2004) when she writes, "[e]ven one person all alone, engaged in a silent or oral reading of ancient scrolls found in a cave on an island in the middle of an ocean is a social and cultural event, a recursive dialogue between author and reader, a virtual communication between the past and the present" (p. 4).

## Acknowledging Both the Cognitive and the Social in Our Literacy Assessment Practices

While designing literacy tasks that demonstrate a more balanced view of literacy learning is one essential strategy for enacting an anti-oppressive literacy education practice, doing so is virtually pointless if we don't also consider and work to disrupt how some of our most common literacy assessments continue to privilege individual cognitive skills over authentic social practices.

## Broadening What Counts as "Data"

One of the ways we can do this is by recognizing the differences between what Shane Safir and Jamila Dugan (2021), the authors of *Street Data: A Next-Generation Model for Equity, Pedagogy, and School Transformation*, call "satellite," "map," and "street" data. Assessment practices that offer educators satellite data, like that most prized by pundits and policy makers, take a broad, bird's-eye view of student learning. This form of data, while useful in particular contexts, "hovers far above the classroom" and "[fails] to take into account . . . the layered, human experiences" that both students and teachers bring to school spaces (p. 56).

Assessment practices that provide us with map data tend to take a slightly less "aerial" view. Satellite- and map-friendly measures of learning (such as standardized, computer-based assessments or on-demand writing prompts) are often norm-referenced or comparative types of measures and are characterized as "snapshots" of what children can do in relatively controlled environments. Alternatively, assessment practices that offer us street data, such as kidwatching, interviews, and locally designed performance assessments, have the potential to be more systematic, nuanced, and—in theory, at least—more culturally responsive, helping illuminate "what's *right* in our students, schools, and communities" (p. 57). When educators rely too heavily on satellite measures of learning, like high-stakes standardized tests, we place unfair and inequitable constraints on what students can demonstrate they know and are able to do.

I consider street data to be more culturally responsive "in theory" because, as Safir and Dugan also point out in their book, educators must also put in the sustained and sometimes challenging work to explore their own identities (and the assumptions and biases that accompany them) in order to ensure that the data that emerges from arguably more subjective assessment practices—e.g., kidwatching—is equitably gained.

| **Table 2.2:** Assessment Practices That Can Offer Us "Street" Data* | |
|---|---|
| **Kidwatching** | Kidwatching is a method of using critically conscious observation, listening, and documentation in order to make students' knowledge visible. Popularized by researchers Yetta and Ken Goodman, such a method of assessment helps educators "develop insight about children's ways of thinking about and understanding the world" (Owocki & Goodman, 2002, p. 3) in order to inform their own understanding (and ultimately, their instruction). |
| **Interviews/ Conferring** | The best interviews or conferences use open-ended questions to gauge what students know, what they are able to do, and what their goals are around their learning. Often, these are accompanied by student work (e.g., a piece of writing in progress) and are conversational in nature. While many reading and writing conferences include an individualized teaching point designed to help build on what the student already knows/is able to do, sometimes the purpose is simply to gather evidence of learning and/or elicit important feedback from the student. |
| **Locally Designed Performance Assessments** | The most well-designed performance assessments offer students the opportunity to demonstrate their learning or acquisition of skills to authentic audiences in a meaningful way. This kind of assessment, unlike what education scholar Linda Darling-Hammond (2014) cheekily calls "bubble tests," honors the social situatedness of literacy learning and offers educators a more broad, multifaceted understanding of who students are as readers, writers, and speakers.<br><br>An example of a performance assessment task would be to invite students to contribute a comic strip to a comic book collection that would then be distributed around the school or community or to invite students to perform their spoken word poems during an intimate (virtual or in-person) open-mic event for families. These kinds of assessment practices, especially when accompanied by student reflection, offer teachers valuable opportunities to observe and/or listen deeply to what students know and are able to do. |

| Literacy Portfolios | Just like any other kind of portfolio, a literacy portfolio is a carefully curated collection of ideas, artifacts, stories, and observations about a particular literacy learner, including their engagement in authentic literacy events. Rather than being a one-time "snapshot" of a given task or a static measure of "proficiency," a literacy portfolio can tell an evolving, multidimensional story of a learner's progress and development over time as a reader, writer, speaker, and listener. |
|---|---|
| | Literacy portfolios were enormously popular when I first became a classroom teacher over two decades ago, and I loved being able to offer my students choice in what to share as well as multiple opportunities to reflect on themselves as learners. However, this was prior to the advent of many of the digital tools that we have access to today, and so helping my students develop their portfolios was quite a challenge to manage (imagine papers would be flying everywhere)! Fortunately, today there are a wide variety of tools that educators can invite students to use to communicate about their learning, including Google Slides, Google Sites, Book Creator, Wakelet, Padlet, Seesaw, and more. |

\* (Safir & Dugan, 2021)

## The "Stories" Our Assessment Practices Tell

The limits of using standardized measures to assess children's literacy learning have been widely documented by a number of literacy researchers and theorists (Afflerbach, 2018; Valencia, 2010; Wiggins, 1993). However, since we are here, let's think about the kinds of questions that are most often asked of students on the vast majority of standardized literacy assessments and the "stories" they tell, or the messages they implicitly send, about what it means to be a proficient reader or writer. On a high-stakes standardized assessment such as the NWEA Measure of Academic Progress (MAP) test or the STAR reading assessment, a fourth-grade student would typically be asked to demonstrate "proficiency" in the following tasks:

- Read a passage (*not* of the child's own choosing), then answer questions about . . .
  - the "main idea" of the passage;

- the author's "purpose" in writing the passage;
- what characters' motivations are;
- what certain words used in the passage mean;
- what additional detail would most improve the passage; and
- where to find specific information in the passage.

- Additionally, a student would very likely be asked to:
  - Choose the correct piece of punctuation to use in a sentence.
  - Select a word or phrase that best completes a sentence.
  - Correct a word-level error in a sentence.

While this list does not encompass everything a student might be asked to do on an assessment like this, it is clear from these examples that a particular set of "stories" about what it means to be a reader and/or a writer is being told via this assessment. These stories include

- that both reading and writing are "in the head," skills-based operations, independent from social or cultural practices;
- that reading is a means to an end, and that "end" is to answer questions that purport to demonstrate the reader's individual understanding of a print text;
- that reading and writing largely involve only print, or alphabetic, texts;
- that the "correct" answer to these questions—and questions like them—is cut-and-dried, leaving little to no room for interpretation or subjectivity;
- that there is a universally acceptable or "standard" way to engage with the English language or to write something that can be comprehended by a culturally and politically "neutral" audience.

What other "stories" do assessments like these "tell" students about what it means to be a reader or writer? Compare this with a reading or writing assessment that is more authentic in nature and that

- is multifaceted (e.g., that includes assessments across a period of time that show evidence of a reader's or writer's interests, processes, and motivations);

- includes both teacher observation and student self-reflection;
- happens in real time (e.g., during a conferring session or presentation);
- includes the application of skills (such as decoding an unfamiliar word, editing a sentence for clarity) within meaningful contexts;
- is progress (as opposed to "achievement") focused.

While more authentic and "on the ground" assessments of student reading and writing practices can be more challenging and time-consuming than those that are more standardized or skills-based, if we are to truly disrupt dominant conceptions of what literacy "is"—and what it means to be a "proficient" reader and/or writer—we must use our political and social capital to advocate for such kinds of assessment *alongside* those that are typically mandated in schools and classrooms—and also for the professional learning necessary to be able to design and implement them effectively.

Far from being a tool for merely sending "implicit" messages about what "counts" as literacy, the traditional literacy assessment, or what linguist James Collins (1989) calls "examinations" in his piece "Hegemonic Practice: Literacy and Standard Language in Public Education," goes so far as to echo the musings of famed philosopher and critic Paul-Michel Foucault, who considered dominant "examinations" that professed to assess one's level of literacy attainment as being "part of a process of gaining knowledge and control over populations" (Collins, 1989, p. 10).

### Internal Work
- Spend some time with Table 2.1, in which I summarize the differences between an autonomous and an ideological model of literacy. Which model best reflects your beliefs about literacy? How, if at all, have your beliefs begun to shift since reading this chapter?
- Building off of some of the "internal work" prompts from the introduction, take a moment to jot a list of your own social and

cultural literacy practices. What specific literacy practices do you engage in most frequently? (Don't judge your jotting—everything "counts"!) How, if at all, were the literacy practices you engaged with as a child reflected in your schooling experience? Which of your practices are granted the most privilege or power in your professional spaces?

## External Work

- If you have not yet done so, make an effort to avail yourself of your students' existing social and cultural literacy practices. What are they? How do you know?
- Make a list of the "stories" that your (and your colleagues') specific literacy instruction and assessment practices "tell" students about literacy. What messages do they send to students about what it means to be a reader or writer? Do these messages match the stories you *want* to tell students? If not, how might you revise your instructional and/or assessment practices in order to make them more authentic and reflective of a wide range of social/cultural literacy practices?
- Continue to jot what you are noticing about where literacy oppression "lives" in your district/school/classroom using the table from Chapter 1 as a guide.

# CHAPTER 3

# Literacy and Identity Are Inextricably Linked

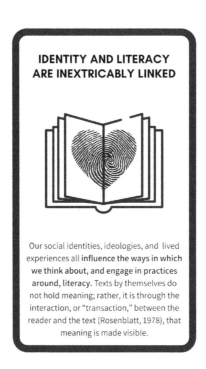

**IDENTITY AND LITERACY ARE INEXTRICABLY LINKED**

Our social identities, ideologies, and lived experiences all **influence the ways in which we think about, and engage in practices around, literacy.** Texts by themselves do not hold meaning; rather, it is through the interaction, or "transaction," between the reader and the text (Rosenblatt, 1978), that meaning is made visible.

*Identity matters; it has always mattered.*
—Dr. Liza A. Talusan (2022), *The Identity-Conscious Educator: Building Habits and Skills for a More Inclusive School*

DOI: 10.4324/9781032658964-3

I closed the book *Black Enough: Stories of Being Young and Black in America*, from which I was reading aloud Jason Reynolds's short story "The Ingredients" to the five White teenagers sitting in front of me and smiled.

Four of them stared back at me. One continued doodling on the piece of scrap paper in front of him.

"So . . . ?" I leaned forward, eager to engage them in a conversation about Reynolds's craft as a writer. "What did you think? Reactions?"

"It was okay," Jenna* replied. "I mean . . . it was . . . pretty good."

*I have used pseudonyms throughout the book in place of students' real names and changed several other details as well for privacy.

"I didn't like it," Lucas announced, leaning back in his chair.

"Tell me more," I said, trying to keep my smile even. I had been sure they would love this story, which follows four friends walking home from the neighborhood pool on a hot summer day, as much as I did.

Kaden looked up at me from his work. "It just wasn't . . . realistic," he said, wrinkling his nose. The others nodded.

"'Realistic' in what way?" I asked.

"No one *talks* like that," Kaden explained. "'Yo, yo. Y'all are *doooope*,'" he intoned, mimicking the characters' dialogue, and laughed. "It's stupid." His classmates listlessly gazed at the table.

The blood drained from my face, and I cleared my throat. "I'm going to ask you not to say 'stupid' when talking about these characters, Kaden," I said, trying not to show how disappointed I was at his response. "But let's all talk about this a little . . ."

## Identity Matters

I spent the remainder of my time that afternoon with my students attempting to explain what educator and activist Dr. April Baker-Bell calls "Black Language" and how it differs from White Mainstream English, or what some inaccurately (and harmfully) call "standard"

American English. I left the learning center where I was teaching that day knowing that not only had I failed the students who were taking my class, I had failed Jason Reynolds and his beloved characters as well by not considering beforehand how important identity is to both reading and writing. How irrevocably intertwined literacy practices are with *how we identify, how we are identified by others*, and *how our identities impact our lived experiences.*

Those students weren't trying to be racist or anti-Black. Regardless, their reaction to the way the characters in "The Ingredients" spoke *was* both of these things. I could, and did, blame myself for not attending to their racial and linguistic identities before deciding to read that particular story aloud. I blamed the schools from where these students came, and the educators they'd had prior to me, for failing to engage them in texts representing a wide variety of characters, languages, and lived experiences. I even blamed the ways in which property taxes in our home state determine district boundaries, creating segregated schools— which, I was convinced, contributed to my students' reactions to the story. As I reflect on that afternoon now, I can visualize driving home in my car, tossing blame around like New Year's Eve confetti. And while it's important for me and others to understand the wide range of systemic, institutional, and interpersonal factors that led up to that moment— and so many other moments like it—simply assigning blame to all of these is not going to change much of anything. However, understanding how exceedingly interconnected identity and literacy practices are *will*.

## But First: What Is Identity?

When most people think of identity, they often think of the ways in which people identify at the individual level. For some, "identity" is frequently conceptualized as a set of characteristics or behaviors: *I am kind. I am a runner. I am a sucker for ice cream.* Sometimes identity is conceptualized through our relationships with others: *I am a mother. A teammate. A student.* While our dynamic characteristics and the ways in which we relate to and interact with others surely make up part of our varied and complex identities, it's also important for us to think more broadly—and at the same time, more deeply—about how we think about who we are.

## ALL MY RELATIONS

The concept of "All My Relations," an important aspect of many First Nations worldviews, is more complex (and comprehensive) than most non-Natives' ideas of interpersonal relations. The Lakota prayer *Mitákuye oyás 'iŋ*, for example, loosely translates to "We are all related," and refers to the interconnectedness of all beings and things beyond family, cultural, or even physical relations. To learn more about what it means, and how the idea manifests in everyday life, check out the All My Relations podcast hosted by Matika Wilbur (Swinomish and Tulalip) and Dr. Adrienne Keene (Cherokee Nation) (https://www.allmyrelationspodcast.com/).

When working with youth and educators around identity, I often take a page from Dr. Beverly Daniel Tatum (2013) and invite them to list, without stopping or judging, their responses to the sentence stem "I am _____" for a full 60 seconds. I then read aloud this excerpt from her brilliant essay "The Complexity of Identity" as she writes about how her own students typically respond to such an invitation. Of the lists her students end up making, Dr. Tatum writes,

> all kinds of trait descriptors are used—*friendly, shy, assertive, intelligent, honest, and so on*—but over the years I have noticed something else. Students of color usually mention their racial or ethnic group: for instance, I am Black, Puerto Rican, Korean American. White students who have grown up in strong ethnic enclaves occasionally mention being Irish or Italian. But in general, White students rarely mention being White. (pp. 6–7)

She goes on to say that "common across these examples is that in the areas where a person is a member of the dominant or advantaged social group, the category is usually not mentioned. . . . *It is taken for granted by them because it is taken for granted by the dominant culture*" (my emphasis).

In the case of the students I referenced at the beginning of the chapter, this "taking for granted" of what characters in stories are "supposed" to sound like was absolutely connected to my and my students' own dominant identities. While I had somewhat of an understanding of my own racial and linguistic identities and how they differed from the characters in Reynolds's story, I had not done the precursory work necessary to help my students develop an awareness of their own racial and linguistic identities. Thus, I can understand how my students, who took for granted the racialized ways in which they used language, perceived the way the characters in "The Ingredients" spoke as "unrealistic." Not only had my students experienced very little racial or linguistic diversity up until that point in their lives, but the vast majority of the spaces they inhabited—including learning spaces—implicitly held up their own dominant language practices as the norm or "standard."

## Two Frameworks for Defining and Expressing Identity

In a bit, we'll dive more deeply into how schools—and in particular, how school literacy spaces—take dominant identities for granted. For now, I'd like to share two frameworks that I have found enormously helpful when considering and interrogating my own complex identities.

### Micro, Meso, and Macro Levels of Identity

The first is one I learned from Gwyn Kirk and Margo Okazawa-Rey (2013) in their chapter called "Identities and Social Locations" from the book *Readings for Diversity and Social Justice*. For many folks, identity is conceived of as both fixed (e.g., definite) and contained at the individual, or personal, level. But as Kirk and Okazawa-Rey explain, identity development happens as a result of "the complex interplay among individual decisions and choices, particular life events, community recognition and expectations, and societal categorization, classification, and socialization" (p. 9). Because of this complexity, identity is ever-changing; there is never a time during our lives when our identities have "finished" forming and evolving.

Figure 3.2 provides a visual representation of these complex interplays. At the core, or micro level, is where we (theoretically) have the most control over our identities—or at least, how we choose to define or express them. It is also where what Kirk and Okazawa-Rey call "critical life events," such as the death of a family member—or an affirming or harmful school experience—can "serve as catalysts" for a shift in our identity. (I sometimes joke, to keep from crying, that this level of identity development is where "villain origin story" was created.) For example, throughout my junior year of high school, I was harassed by a popular (and thus socially powerful) group of boys, who would loudly comment on my body in the hallways and ask me for sexual favors in front of my classmates. When I protested loudly and sought support from my teachers and administrators around this, I was roundly criticized for "making a big deal" out of nothing and for potentially "jeopardizing" the future life prospects of my harassers. The previous fall, attorney Anita Hill had testified during a televised Senate hearing that she had been sexually harassed by her then employer, Supreme Court nominee (and now judge) Clarence Thomas. These combined events

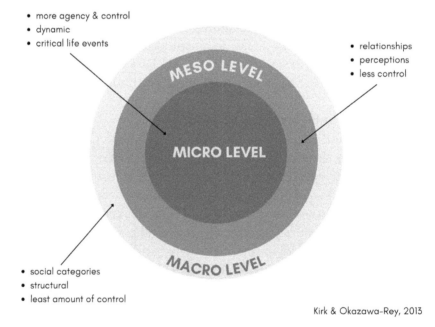

- more agency & control
- dynamic
- critical life events

- relationships
- perceptions
- less control

MESO LEVEL

MICRO LEVEL

MACRO LEVEL

- social categories
- structural
- least amount of control

Kirk & Okazawa-Rey, 2013

**Figure 3.2**  "Levels" of Identity

are what first compelled me to identify as a feminist, and I began to look carefully at the ways in which women were, and are, often dismissed, denigrated, or ridiculed in our society. It was also, for better or worse, when I first began to understand how my body and the way I dressed could either attract or discourage attention, depending on how I decided to express myself.

## INTERSECTIONALITY

While as an adolescent I was beginning to form conceptions of what I now understand as systemic and/or institutional oppression—in this case, the oppression of women—I had yet to understand how this plays out differently for women with different social identities. For example, as inspired as I was by Dr. Anita Hill's courageous testimony, I was unable to "see" how her experience was complicated both by her own Blackness and by that of her employer's—and how rooted in misogynoir* Thomas's harassment of her was. Thanks to the work of Dr. Kimberlé Crenshaw (1989) and her conceptualization of "intersectionality," which she defines as a lens through which to consider the ways in which individuals are "multiply burdened" by systemic oppression that "cannot be understood as resulting from discrete sources of discrimination" (e.g., racism, sexism, etc.), I now have a more complex, if still developing, understanding of how systems of oppression work.

*misogynoir* = misogyny directed specifically toward Black women (Bailey & Trudy, 2018)

Kelly Yang (2019), award-winning author of books for middle and high schoolers (*Front Desk, Parachutes*), has shared numerous times how her experience of being bullied at school for her East Asian features and the way she dressed caused her to seek "friends" in books and to deal with her pain through writing: "If my psyche and whole spirit was in a story," she says in one video she's posted to her website, "[the bullies] could not get to me . . . and . . . I found that that was such a great way to have an outlet." that Yang's identity at this micro level shifted from what it was at an earlier age due to the harassment she endured, leading her to eventually write stories whose characters deal with some of the very issues she did as a young girl.

The meso level is where our identities are formed as a result of our relationship to others and to varying communities (both literal and metaphorical). At this level, Kirk and Okazawa-Rey (2013) write, individuals typically have less agency due to the fact that "individual identities and needs" may or may not "meet group standards, expectations, obligations, responsibilities, and demands" (p. 11). This is where others' perceptions of us influence how our identities are shaped. For example, while I identify as queer, and have for many years, my degree of "outness" is not such that I (at the time of this writing) feel wholly a part of any queer communities. This is both due to my own actions and behaviors—or lack of—within certain groups as well as how others perceive me, particularly knowing that I am in a long-term marriage with a cishet male partner (despite this having nothing to do with how "queer" or "not queer" I am). Regardless, I feel a strong affinity with queer folks and share many of the same goals and interests as those in a number of queer communities.

In traditional Black literary societies, according to scholars Detra Price-Dennis, Gholdy Muhammad, Erica Womack, Sherell A. McArthur, and Marcelle Haddix, literacy itself served as an identity-defining tool for those who participated. This was particularly the case for young Black women, the authors write:

> As they were reading text, [these women] were not only discussing their collective identities as Black women, but also their individual and unique self-identities. Their engagements in reading, writing, speaking and thinking were intertwined with, and never isolated from, their pursuits to define their lives. (Price-Dennis et al., 2017, p. 3)

Knowing how the meso level of identity is intimately connected to our relations with others, we educators, as members of school-based literacy and learning communities, must be exceedingly mindful of how we perceive, and thus interact with, the students we have within our care. Too often, deficit-based views of students' literacy and language practices lead to their marginalization within classroom spaces, which can have profound impacts on their identity development both within and outside of these spaces.

Finally, the macro or global level is where our identities shift and change as a result of social categories and constructs. This is where we as individuals have the *least* control/agency, where our identities feel the *least* dynamic, and where we are subject to "the structural inequalities present in our society . . . [where] group[s] of people [are] deemed superior, legitimate, dominant, and privileged while others are relegated—whether explicitly or implicitly—to the position of inferior, illegitimate, subordinate, and disadvantaged" (Kirk & Okazawa-Rey, p. 12).

### The Wheel of Power/ Privilege

This last particular level of identity becomes clearer when we consider another tool I find useful, called the Wheel of Power/Privilege (WPP). Originally created by folks at the Canadian Council for Refugees and based upon the work of Rick Arnold, Bev Burke, Carl James, D'Arcy Martin, and Barb Thomas (1991) in their book *Educating for a Change*, the WPP, as conceptualized by Toronto educator Sylvia Duckworth (Figure 3.3), is a visual representation of how identity and power are intertwined. In the center of the wheel are the identities or attributes that are traditionally granted the most power in society: White, heterosexual, able-bodied, light skinned, and so forth. Moving out from the wheel's center are identities or attributes that have historically been, and continue to be, marginalized or disenfranchised (e.g., non-White, queer, disabled, dark skinned, etc.). Placed around the perimeter of the WPP are identity categories, most of which are social, rather than biological, constructs—race, sexuality, gender, and the like.

This particular tool, while imperfect, is helpful when considering the many complex identities we have—or *that we are perceived as having*—and how these either confer power or confer disadvantage to us as we move about in the world. For example, it's no surprise

**Figure 3.3**   Wheel of Power/Privilege
Source: Sylvia Duckworth.

to most people that one's citizenship status can have an impact on what individuals are able to obtain in terms of employment, health care, housing, higher education, and so on. Perhaps more surprisingly to some, this is also the case when we think about body size and how dominant ideas about what constitutes an acceptable or so-called "healthy" body size can confer advantage to some and cause great harm and disadvantage to others, something that activists like Jessamyn Stanley (@mynameisjessamyn), Aubrey Gordon (@yrfatfriend), and Caleb Luna (@dr_chairbreaker) have consistently argued. So now that we have familiarized ourselves with how this tool works, let's think about what the concepts of identity, power, and privilege mean when it comes to students' experiences in school spaces, particularly literacy spaces.

## LIMITATIONS OF THE WHEEL OF POWER/PRIVILEGE

As useful as this image is, I feel compelled to acknowledge its limitations so as not to perpetuate any misunderstandings about how oppression, based upon one's identities, works. For one, it's important to remember the positionality of its illustrator, Sylvia Duckworth, who is both White and Canadian. Some of the ways she has delineated the level of power and/or oppression that some of the identities depicted here experience—which of course are much more dynamic and fluid than this wheel implies—may not be reflective of the perspectives of folks with different identities or who are from other communities.

In addition, some of the ways that how power works when considering intersectionality are also more nuanced than what is represented here. For example, an individual who is both undocumented and White, as is the case with many Ukrainian refugees (to use a current example), often experiences a much greater level of power and privilege than an individual who is both undocumented and *not* White. Also, some looking at this tool would argue that folks who identify as bisexual experience greater power and privilege than gay men do and not the other way around, as Duckworth's wheel represents. Regardless of its flaws, I do find her representation to be a powerful catalyst for discussion around notions of identity and power and am grateful for her permission to use it here.

Some questions we might consider posing to a group of students or colleagues around this wheel, or one similar to it, include:

- What do you *notice* about the identities that are represented here? What do you wonder?
- What kinds of identities are *missing* here (e.g., Indigeneity)? What would you add to this wheel?
- What do you *agree with* here, based on your own lived experience? What do you *disagree with*?
- Compare this wheel with other, similar wheels that folks have created. Which ones do you find to be *most accurate* or *representative* of how identity and power work together? Why?

- If given the opportunity, how would *you* visually represent the relationships among identity, power, and privilege?

## Identity and the Texts That We Value

As I argued in Chapter 2, the literacy practices in which individuals engage within school spaces, even those that are cognitive in nature, must be contextualized within larger social and cultural contexts. There is no "neutral" when it comes to teaching and learning within these spaces, regardless of how fervently we might argue (or wish) otherwise. This includes, of course, the kinds of texts we use to teach children to read and to write.

Many education colleagues I admire—Angie Manfredi, Chad Everett, Julia Torres, and others—have written or spoken extensively about the ways in which the texts we choose to use in our schools and classrooms send a particular message to students and families about the kinds of identities that are deemed worthy both in and outside of our classroom walls. You may have heard of Dr. Rudine Sims Bishop's (1990) call for educators to offer children access, through texts, to "mirrors, windows, and sliding glass doors" that allow them to see not only *themselves* but *others* represented in histories. She writes:

> *When children cannot find themselves reflected in the books they read, or when the images they see are distorted, negative, or laughable, they learn a powerful lesson about how they are devalued in the society of which they are a part.*

She goes on to say that

> *children from dominant groups . . . need books that will help them understand the multicultural nature of the world they live in, and their place as a member of just one group, as well as their connections to all other humans. (para. 5)*

For too long, the stories and experiences of those who hold dominant identities—and thus those with the most power in society—have been centered in schools and classrooms. Not too long ago, a colleague and I were hired as consultants at an urban charter school serving students in grades K–6. Our charge was to help the faculty and staff engage in more culturally sustaining literacy pedagogies in order to help its educators more effectively engage their students in literacy practices (and, of course, raise their standardized test scores). Partly because it's always much more comfortable to begin by looking critically at *texts* than at *people and practices*, one of the first things my colleague and I did was to invite members of the faculty and staff to choose a unit from the required literacy program they were using at the time and conduct a brief "audit" of all of the texts included in that unit. Among other things, we asked them to document the following information:

- a photo of each author whose work was featured in the unit;
- a photo of the cover of each text (if applicable); and
- the copyright date of each text included in the unit.

As members of that school's faculty and staff began plugging this data into the table we had created for them, they quickly realized that, in most of the units within the literacy program they were using,

- the vast majority of authors their students were being exposed to were White;
- the vast majority of the *main characters* within the books/stories they were using were White; and
- the most contemporary texts included in the unit were anywhere from 20 to 30 years old.

This data posed a huge problem, especially considering that the school served anywhere from 90% to 95% Black children. Where, we asked, were these children seeing their identities and experiences reflected in the texts they were being asked to read? What messages were these texts, almost all of which could be classified as "windows" in this particular context, sending these students about whose stories, ideas, and

**Table 3.1** Text "Audit" Tool

UNIT and/or TEXT SET:

| Title of text, author, illustrator | Text form and/or genre | Photo of author and/or known identities | Copyright date | Identities of main character(s) (if known) | Main topic, theme, or story line | Main instructional use(s) (e.g., to teach a particular literacy skill or writing craft move) | Alternative or supplemental text(s) (e.g., counternarratives) that could be used for a similar use |
|---|---|---|---|---|---|---|---|
| | | | | | | | |
| | | | | | | | |
| | | | | | | | |
| | | | | | | | |
| | | | | | | | |
| | | | | | | | |
| | | | | | | | |
| | | | | | | | |

WHAT DO YOU *NOTICE?*

WHAT DO YOU *WONDER?*

experiences *matter* in the world? While my colleague and I were not at all surprised by what we discovered in facilitating this text audit with this particular school, it was difficult not to feel disheartened by the fact that this was still happening in schools in 2021.

Text sets like the ones this particular school was using are surely harmful to Black and Brown children. They are additionally harmful, though arguably to a much lesser degree, to students who are White, who continue to receive the message, perpetuated by much of the media they consume outside of school, that *their* histories, *their* experiences, and *their* lives matter most. In their book *What If All the Kids Are White*, Louise Derman-Sparks and Patricia G. Ramsey (2011) note that

> *in contrast to their peers of color, White children receive a barrage of messages from society that reinforces their positive group identity. . . . [T]he dynamics of systemic racial advantage and disadvantage provide fertile ground for all White children to highly value their Whiteness, and to develop a sense of racial superiority. (p. 47)*

## TEXT AUDITS ARE NOT ENOUGH

While engaging colleagues (or students!) in a text audit can be a good first step in interrupting the ways that dominant identities are centered in school literacy spaces, we need to move beyond such surface-level work and consider both

- how to build capacity around engaging both colleagues and students in critical dialogue regarding text selection, reading and writing identities, and which histories and experiences are privileged in texts; and
- how to move beyond texts and both explore and disrupt the ways in which the institution of schooling, and our system of education (of which *we play a part*), creates the environment that leads to this centering of dominant identities.

Some of my favorite texts that address one or both of these issues include the following:

"Got Diverse Texts? Now What? Teachers as Critical Guides in the Moment" by Tiffany M. Nyachae (*Literacy Today*, May/June 2021)

"Disrupting Your Texts: Why Simply Including Diverse Voices Is Not Enough" by Tricia Ebarvia (*Literacy Now*, September 2019)

"Foggy Mirrors, Tiny Windows, and Heavy Doors: Beyond Diverse Books Toward Meaningful Literacy Instruction" by Grace Enriquez (*The Reading Teacher*, July/August 2021)

## Beyond Racial and Ethnic Identity

This issue of "too many windows and not enough mirrors," or vice versa, is not particular to race or ethnicity—although it does, on the surface, seem to be where the most glaring oppression occurs. For example, I can name on one hand the number of texts I read in school that included the experiences of disabled, neurodivergent, undocumented, Indigenous, queer, or poor individuals. And if they were included, they were taught or made available not within my "core" classes but rather in electives my high school offered that had titles like "Minority Literature". If I had been exposed to a wider, more inclusive range of histories and experiences, I can't help but wonder if I would have felt more comfortable and confident in my own queerness and neurodivergency as a child/adolescent. I also can't help but wonder what I would have gained earlier in life by being invited to engage with a more diverse range of texts in my core classes. But I was denied that opportunity, just as so many children and youth continue to be denied that opportunity through the overvaluing of dominant narratives in the texts we share with students, whether through read-alouds, book talks, or mentor texts for writing.

Being a White, cisgender, able-bodied woman with an enormous amount of power and privilege in this world, I came away from my K–12 schooling experience relatively unscathed—to put it mildly. This is not, of course, the case for those whose identities are traditionally conferred *less* privilege and power. In an essay she wrote for the blog series *#31DaysIBPOC*, created in 2019 by Tricia Ebarvia and Dr. Kim

Parker, teacher and author Lisa Stringfellow, who is Black, reflects on her experience attending an affluent Boston-area school:

> *Growing up in the 1970s and 80s, if I found a book by a Black author in my elementary and middle school libraries, it was usually historical or realistic fiction. Often it didn't reflect the middle class family and environment in which I lived. I wanted to write something different. A book that "middle-school-me" would have curled under the covers with a flashlight to read. A book where a girl like me could see herself on a magical adventure. (2019, para. 26)*

In a 2016 TEDx Talk, Grace Lin, award-winning children's book author and illustrator, reflects on her experience growing up Chinese in predominantly White upstate New York:

> *In a lot of ways, it was really easy to forget [that I was Asian]. It seemed like there was nobody that looked like me anywhere. There was nobody that looked like me in school, there was nobody that looked like me in the movies, there was nobody that looked like me on TV or in the magazines . . . and most importantly, there was nobody that looked like me in the books that I loved. (2:31)*

For Lin, the only book she and her classmates saw in school that *did* represent her—her ethnicity, anyway—was Claire Huchet Bishop's 1938 book *The Five Chinese Brothers*, a trade book appropriated from Chinese folklore (without attribution) in which the characters are illustrated in a way that is undeniably racist.

Grace's experience as a young girl is illustrative of the importance of reaching higher than the low-hanging fruit that is "diverse" or "inclusive" representation within the texts we use and share with students. What good is the inclusive representation of a wide variety of identities within texts if that representation serves only to perpetuate stereotypes? Julie Stivers (2015), a librarian and author who is committed to building inclusive school spaces, asks these questions of her colleagues in a post she wrote for Dr. Debbie Reese's blog *American Indians in Children's Literature*:

*Let's think for a moment about the books we own that feature Native American main characters. What are their settings? In the past? Modern day? If the text does not make this clear—if, for example, there are anthropomorphic animals—what are they wearing? Baseball caps and modern clothes or "leather and feathers"? (para. 1)*

Stiver points to the dangers of prevalent narratives within children's literature, like those depicting Indigenous folks as "people of the past," which, as she writes, "puts forth a narrative that Native American people *themselves* are only of the past, allowing their present lives—and their sovereign rights—to be ignored" (para. 2). If we were to extend this beyond racial—or racialized—identities, we would need to ask ourselves questions like the following:

- Of the texts we have that feature neurodivergent or disabled individuals/characters, how many are *not* centered on the struggles they face in various spaces?
- Of the texts that feature transgender individuals/characters, how many are *not* centered around their transness?
- Of the texts that feature fat individuals/characters, how many are *not* centered around their body or their "worth" as romantic or sexual partners?

These questions are important because, while it is of course essential that we invite our students to engage with texts that *do* deal with social issues and struggle, it is equally important to engage them in texts that represent a wide variety of characters or individuals who are *simply living their lives*—where they are not always reduced to their marginalized identities.

### A NOTE ON TERMINOLOGY

While the use of the term "fat" may surprise some readers, or cause some readers discomfort, I am honoring the efforts of many fat activists

and members of the "fat acceptance" community, such as those I mentioned earlier, by choosing to use the word as a descriptor (over, say,
"overweight" or "large-bodied") in order to help destigmatize the term.

## Identity and the Literacy Practices We Value

While it's relatively easy to see how identity-based oppression can
play out in terms of the kinds of books and other texts we privilege in
schools and classrooms, it's less easy, I think, to consider how this plays
out in terms of the literacy *practices* that we value.

### Who We Identify as "Readers" or "Writers"

Let's consider, for example, how both teachers' and students' social
identities within the wider world and their school-based literacy identities intersect. I've mentioned before that partially due to the fact that
my own literacy and language practices outside of school matched those
that are typically privileged in school spaces (e.g., reading novels, being
read to, writing stories, etc.), I was identified early on as both a "reader"
and a "writer" by the teachers and other adults that surrounded me. In
fact, at age 5 I was placed in the "gifted" program at my elementary
school, where the other "gifted" students and I—all White girls—spent
time working on extended research projects that consisted of an enormous number of reading and writing tasks, including the reading and
writing of informational texts. (Personally, I remember just wanting
to stay with my class during their daily read-alouds!) These attributes
that were bestowed upon me early on by the adults in charge—those
whom I naturally perceived as being "in the know"—had an enormous
effect on how I myself identified; I can't remember a time after age 5
when I *didn't* think of myself as a reader or a writer. My teachers and
other adults around me *said* I was a reader and a writer—a gifted one,
at that!—and so the descriptor stuck.

I say all this not to brag about how fabulous my teachers thought
I was but to highlight how: (1) educators' ideas about reading and

writing identity (e.g., who is deemed "a reader" or "a writer") can influence students' own perceptions of themselves as literate beings, and (2) the alignment—or misalignment—of individuals' in-school and out-of-school identities, and their attendant literacy practices, can play an enormous role in these perceptions.

## The Language We Use to Label Students

In a synthesis of three separate studies literacy researcher Leigh A. Hall and her colleagues (2009) conducted around how literacy identities are constructed and enacted in school spaces, the authors concluded that the teachers' descriptions of what it meant to be a "good"

| **Table 3.2:** Dominant Conceptions of Reading/ Writing Identities* | |
|---|---|
| A *reader* is someone who . . . | A *writer* is someone who . . . |
| • reads often | • writes often |
| • reads books (esp. chapter books) | • writes mostly alphabetic forms of text (e.g., stories, essays, poetry) |
| • can adequately comprehend what they read | |
| • reads outside of school | • uses so-called "appropriate" grammar, mechanics, etc. |
| • enjoys reading | • enjoys writing |
| • is aware of what strategies they use while reading | • employs "craft" in their writing |
| • can read for a sustained length of time | • can write for a sustained length of time |

*Based on my own 23+ years of experience as a literacy educator

or "poor" reader "told students what it meant to be literate" and "influenced students' beliefs about *who they were* or *could become* as readers" (p. 31; my emphasis). These descriptions, which included notions around how well readers understood how much of what they read, how likely they were to use comprehension strategies or not, and so on, placed students in the position of "tak[ing] on the identities presented by their teachers, and receive[ing] praise, or opt[ing] for ones less valued and risk marginalization" (p. 33). Too often, this marginalization comes in the form of being labeled "at risk," as being "in need of intervention," or as a "struggling" or "reluctant" reader and/or writer, depending on how seamlessly one's literacy practices align with those sanctioned in school spaces. (And in some classrooms, one's reading identity can even be reduced to a *single letter or number* based upon how they perform on certain reading assessments; e.g., when being assessed via the Fountas and Pinnell Benchmark Assessment or the Developmental Reading Assessment.)

## LETTING GO OF STUDENT LABELS

In her dissertation, titled *Breaking the "At Risk" Code: Deconstructing the Myth and the Label*, Kara Christine Allen (2014) writes that "within the educational sector, there exist endless acronyms and jargon used by professionals in the field" to sort and divide students "from the mainstream" (p. 3). You may have, as have I, at one time or another used some of the most common of these to label students as "at risk," "reluctant," "struggling," "gifted," or "advanced." (In social media spaces, it is also not uncommon to see teachers identify themselves as a "Title 1 teacher" or as working with "Title 1 kids.") As Allen and others (Cuban, 1989; Placier, 1996) argue, there are a number of problems that are associated with these socially and politically constructed labels. Most severe among them, however, is the way in which they both perpetuate deficit views of children and center dominant notions of academic "success" and/or "proficiency," which, Allen writes, "diverts attention away from systemic deficiencies that are the central cause of the problems in the first place" (p. 8).

Jacqueline Woodson, award-winning author and 2018–2019 National Ambassador for Young People's Literature, has also used her platform to advocate against the use of these kinds of terms to label children and youth. In a 2018 interview for *Education Week*, she explains that, indeed,

> *any kind of qualifier [about who we are as learners] can be harmful because who we are is not static. Our abilities are constantly changing. . . . I know if I was raised in this day and age, I would have been labeled a struggling reader. But what I know now is I was actually reading like a writer. I was reading slowly and deliberately and deconstructing language, not in the sense of looking up words in the dictionary, but understanding from context. I was constantly being compared to my sister who excelled, and it made me feel insecure. What gets translated is "you are not as good," and that gets trans-lated into our whole bodies. That's where the danger lies.*

## Avoiding Deficit Thinking

In her piece "Positioning Students as Readers and Writers through Talk in a High School English Classroom," Dr. Amy Vetter (2010) discusses some of the ways that educators might avoid this kind of marginalization or deficit framing based on a five-month qualitative study following one high school English teacher, Gina, whose students represented a range of racial, ethnic, and linguistic identities and who, through their ongoing interactions with their teacher, "eventually took up engaged and capable positions" as readers and writers (p. 44). Dr. Vetter identified several moves that educators could make in order to help students nurture their own positive reader and writer identities, among them

- inviting students to co-construct classroom literacy events based upon their needs and interests;
- shifting the alignment of power in the classroom (e.g., from direc-tor to facilitator) whenever possible in order to provide students

with opportunities to build and share knowledge in ways that honor their varying social identities;

- offering students alternative forms of participating in literacy events; for example, by providing choice in what, how, and/or when they engage with them;
- encouraging students to draw from their past experiences as readers, writers, and speakers—including those that may not be traditionally valued in school spaces—in order to help them build new knowledge and develop new literacy practices;
- noticing and naming the effective reading and writing moves that students make, both in conferring conversations and in larger group discussions.

These moves echo those often suggested by language scholars such as Dr. Lisa Delpit (2002), who has written that it's not students' language practices that cause "problems" in school, but rather "the educational bureaucracy's *response to*" their language practices (p. xxiii; my emphasis). Dr. Kris Gutiérrez, another language scholar I admire, has long theorized a dynamic "third space" that exists between students' community/home language practices and "the 'color [evasive]' practices of English-only, one-size-fits-all curricula and policies and practices driven by high-stakes assessment" (2008, p. 148) and in which "the potential for authentic interaction and learning [can] occur" (1997, p. 372). In this space, Gutiérrez (1997) writes,

- both students' and teachers' language is "consciously at the center of learning" (p. 372);
- classrooms embody a "shift in foci from teaching to learning, from individuals to collectives, from classrooms to communities, and from habitual to reflexive practice" (p. 372);
- teachers recognize and celebrate "the richness of the linguistic repertoires available in the classroom" (p. 374); and
- there exists a "dynamic nature of the roles of teacher and student, and of novice and expert" within the learning space (p. 373).

In this same spirit, Jennifer Scoggin and Hannah Schneewind (2021), literacy educators and coauthors of the book *Trusting Readers*, recommend an inquiry-based model for authentically uncovering students' reading identities called a Discovery Conference, positioning teachers as learners and practitioners of reflection as they "get to know and reknow [students] and their evolving reading identities" (p. 79) over the course of a 5-to-10-minute conversation. Such a conference includes open-ended prompts and questions like, "Tell me about yourself as a reader" and "What makes you stick with a book?"—all of which can be easily modified to use with student writers as well. The entire template for the Discovery Conference can be downloaded for free at https://www.heinemann.com/products/e12047.aspx under the heading "Companion Resources."

It is important to note that engaging in these kinds of practices *alone* will not help students successfully negotiate their identities in a way that will affirm their membership in school-based literacy communities, nor will they entirely mitigate the ways in which dominant identities are privileged in school spaces. In addition to this, we educators must make a committed effort to (1) interrogate how our *own* social identities and experiences have shaped our literacy histories, (2) examine our ideas and assumptions around what it means to be a "reader" and a "writer," and (3) recognize the myriad of ways in which we (both explicitly *and* implicitly) communicate these ideas to students.

### Internal Work

- Think back to your childhood/youth. In what ways *were you identified*—or not identified—as a reader/writer? How did you *self-identify*? How did your reading/writing identity impact your literacy practices, both in and outside of school? How did it impact you overall as a person?
- Using the Wheel of Power/Privilege (or a similar tool), identify the places where your social identities and your identity as a reader and/or writer intersected as a child (or continue to intersect as an adult). What do you notice or wonder about this?

## External Work

- Consider partnering with a trusted colleague (e.g., a classroom teacher, a specialist) to document the patterns of interaction you have with your students over a period of time—over a class period, a day, or even a series of weeks. (*This can be a super scary proposition—I get it!—but I have found this kind of work to be invaluable to me as an educator over the years.*) What do you notice? In looking at overall patterns, what do your interactions explicitly or implicitly "tell" students about themselves as readers and writers? Do these "stories" match your intention or overall goals related to enacting an anti-oppressive practice? If not, what changes need to be made?

- Conduct—and/or invite your students to conduct—a text audit of your curriculum, classroom, or other school space (such as the most public-facing display of your school's library). Whose stories, knowledges, and identities are centered? Whose are not? What can be done to make these spaces more inclusive and representative of a wide variety of identities?

- Continue to jot what you are noticing about where literacy oppression "lives" in your district/school/classroom using the table from Chapter 1 as a guide. What patterns are emerging?

# CHAPTER 4

# All Human Beings Engage in Literacy and Language Practices That Are Both Valid and Valuable

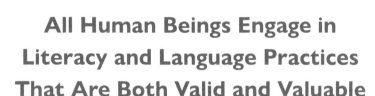

ALL HUMAN BEINGS ENGAGE IN LITERACY & LANGUAGE PRACTICES THAT ARE BOTH VALID AND VALUABLE

Despite what so many have been socialized to believe, and what we are implicitly taught in the majority of school spaces, **there is no one universal way to be literate;** each of us is "highly literate in at least one…context" (Carter, 2006).

*The problem of skill differences among children at the time of school entry is bigger, more intractable, and more important than we had thought. So much is happening to children during their first three years at home, at a time when they are especially malleable, . . . that by age 3, an intervention must address not just a lack of knowledge or skill, but an entire general approach to experience.*

—Betty Hart and Todd L. Risley (2003), "The Early Catastrophe: The 30 Million Word Gap by Age 3"*

DOI: 10.4324/9781032658964-4

(*Note to readers: Before you panic over the quote I've chosen to feature here, read on!)

As a new teacher, I—of *course*—wanted the best for my students. I wanted them to have an equal chance at acquiring the literacy skills necessary for being successful in the world. I was grateful for the (new to me) Response to Intervention model that would provide my students with the literacy intervention they "needed" before making a determination about their qualification for special education. I was full to the brim with both high expectations and "good intentions."

## Unmasking Oppression

[*record scratch*] Okay. Having read Chapters 1–3 of this book, let's take a quick break and unpack that first paragraph for a minute. What's problematic about it? Where might oppression be hiding?

If you've been laser focused on what you've read of this book so far and have begun the internal work necessary for embodying an anti-oppressive literacy practice, you may have picked up on the following:

- My use of the word "equal." *Equal* means that everyone gets the same thing, regardless of their particular needs or interests. Instead, we should be advocating for students to have *equitable* opportunities and access.
- My use of the word "acquiring" in the phrase "*acquiring* the literacy skills necessary." When we *acquire* something, we imply that we are finished; that there is no more work left to do. "Acquiring" also implies that students have nothing to begin with—that they are blank slates. Perhaps "continuing to develop" would have been more appropriate.
- My emphasis on literacy "skills." If we think back to Chapter 1, the notion of literacy being *solely* about a set of discrete skills, and not *also* a variety of evolving social practices, negates the ways in which our identities, cultural ways of being, and lived experiences influence learning.

- My use of the word "successful." What exactly does it mean to be "successful in the world"? It is important to question whose notions of success are being centered when we use this term.
- And finally, this phrase: "provide my students with the literacy intervention they needed." This screams *deficit lens*. In many instances, it's not the *students* who need intervention, but the *policies, practices, attitudes, assumptions,* and *curricula* that need intervening.

## The Harm Embedded in "Word Gap" Discourse

Let's now circle back to the quote featured at the start of this chapter. Many of us, at one time or another, have heard of the so-called 30 million word gap. Perhaps you've read the infamous 1995 Hart and Risley study. After observing, recording, and analyzing thousands of verbal interactions between young children and their caregivers over the course of two and a half years, the researchers who designed this study interpreted their data to have demonstrated that there was a "considerable range in vocabulary size" among children in families of varying income groups. Furthermore, they determined that the measures they used to assess children's range of vocabulary "predicted measures of language skill" at ages 9 and 10 (2003, p. 8).

---

### STOP CITING THE "WORD GAP" STUDY (PLEASE!)

Beyond the problematic (and frankly, racist, classist, and ableist) framing of children and their families that exists within both the design of Hart and Risley's study and the discussion of their findings, many critics of the study have pointed to its small sample size and its inability to be replicated to any significant degree (Kamenetz, 2018). In addition, some language scholars (e.g., Douglas E. Sperry, Linda L. Sperry, and Peggy J. Miller) take issue with the way the researchers collected and interpreted their data, arguing that, in their own similar study,

*when more expansive definitions of the verbal environment were employed . . . the evidence pointed in a different direction. Not only did the Word Gap disappear, but also some poor and working-class communities showed an advantage in the number of words children heard, compared with middle-class communities. (Sperry et al., 2019, p. 1313)*

Despite the barrage of criticism aimed at Hart and Risley's study, the 30 million word gap continues to be cited and used to drive policies and practices at state, district, and school levels.

To learn more about why the Word Gap study is problematic, check out Episode 24 of one of my favorite podcasts, *The Vocal Fries*, with hosts Megan Figueroa and Carrie Gillon and special guest Dr. Nelson Flores (https://radiopublic.com/the-vocal-fries-GooXdO/s1!ce6cf).

As many scholars (Alim & Paris, 2015; Figueroa, 2021; N. Flores, 2018) have spent an enormous amount of time, energy, and labor pointing out, this study is enormously flawed for a variety of reasons. Chief among them is the assumption of both Hart and Risley about the "quality" of the words heard by children from so-called "professional" families versus those from "working-class" or "welfare" families. (Yes, they actually used the term "welfare families.") At one point, the authors write, "We were not surprised to see the 42 children [in our study] turn out to be like their parents; we had not fully realized, however, the implications of those similarities for the children's futures" (p. 3). This study, which has been shared by millions of educators all over the world and has spawned a great number of expensive literacy intervention programs designed to "change the lives" of poor children, is a case study in the kinds of harm that can be caused by using a deficit lens with which to assess the language and literacy practices of individuals and communities that do not match those typically valued in schools.

Describing the bipartisan support of nationwide initiatives intent on closing the "word gap," Dr. Nelson Flores writes, "The one thing that people on both sides of the aisle can apparently agree on is that low-income children of color are linguistically deficient and in need of fixing" (2018, para. 2).

## The Devaluing of Children's Literacy and Language Practices in School Spaces

As the word gap study and its implications for practice have demonstrated, this view of students and their culturally and linguistically variable language practices begins early on in their school lives. READY! For Kindergarten, a program developed through The Children's Reading Foundation of Kennewick, Washington, uses a bold banner on its website to proclaim that "every year, 4 out of 10 kids are already behind on the first day of kindergarten" (Children's Reading Foundation, 2015). In the booklet that they offer as a free download to educators and families, they write that their roster of workshops and accompanying "kits," which seek to "[create] consistency for the child between home and preschool or child care settings," significantly improve children's kindergarten testing scores, with many entering school "testing at or above kindergarten readiness levels" (Children's Reading Foundation, n.d., pp. 9–11). What often remains unspoken and unacknowledged among these kinds of proclamations are the questions of *whose language practices* are held as the "standard" or "norm," and *whose* are most often assessed to be deficient or "behind."

Despite the general silence around this—particularly from publishing houses and other corporations that make their living off of perpetuating "gap" and "readiness" discourse (so as to sell more books and intervention programs, naturally)—it's not actually a mystery whose literacy and language practices are most often held up as the norm in schools and are thus positioned as being the most "valued" and/or "valid," as I've pointed out in previous chapters.

### Learning From the Labor of Our Colleagues of Color

The work of many literacy and language scholars, particularly scholars of color, bears this out. Dr. María Paula Ghiso, associate professor of literacy education at Teachers College, Columbia University, has pointed out that "often, schools are organized in monolingual and monocultural ways that don't necessarily honor the diversities of children's lived realities," including those from (im)migrant backgrounds.

This includes the proliferation of (1) instructional literacy practices that perpetuate the dominance of "standard" English usage, (2) the limited literacy practices most often assessed on high-stakes standardized assessments, and (3) dual language programs that "valorize bilingual practices"—which, as Dr. Ghiso argues, "may not necessarily reflect many young children's transnational experiences, their hybrid language and literacy practices, and the blended nature of their social worlds" (2016, p. 2).

## WHAT ARE "TRANSNATIONAL LITERACIES"?

"Transnational" literacies, a term first coined by literary theorist Gayatri Chakravorty Spivak (1992), is another way of framing the contextual (and often, colonialist) nature of literacy and its attendant practices, particularly as they transcend and/or intersect across social, geographical, and even textual boundaries. For example, the children in Dr. Ghiso's 2016 study engaged in literacy practices that drew upon their varied experiences and knowledges as members of an immigrant community and that offered them the opportunity to compose multimodal texts that reflected these experiences and knowledges. In addition, the children were encouraged to make use of "all the languages they knew" to convey what they wanted to about their community and family lives.

In her research on the literacy practices of 103 emergent bilingual first graders, almost all of whom identify as "Latino," Ghiso found that when the children's experiences were regarded "as rich sites of intellectual inquiry, not merely as a bridge to 'real' academic learning," and their "fluid language practices"—which transcended the boundaries of in-school and out-of-school spaces—were recognized and incorporated into curricular invitations, "the complexity of [the children's] literacy practices" were illuminated (p. 34). In many classrooms, however, either the bridge between students' in-school and out-of-school literacy practices is not considered, or such a bridge is seen as a tool with which to complete a one-way journey—the destination being the assimilation of students' home and community literacy and language practices into those most privileged by schools (i.e., White, Euro-American, English-speaking practices). In their chapter titled "Do You Hear What I Hear? Raciolinguistic Ideologies and Culturally Sustaining Pedagogies," Drs. Jonathan Rosa and Nelson Flores (2017) write that

> *for students of color, the goal of language education is the mastery of mainstream spoken and written language norms. This is one of the ways in which the thinking that students of color "should conform to White, middle-class social norms and identity representations persists (Ladson-Billings, 1999, p. 196). . . . Such "one way" or "assimilate into Whiteness" thinking continually places the onus on students of color to modify their behavior so that they embody appropriateness. (p. 176)*

## Language and Anti-Blackness

This is, of course, not merely the case for immigrant children whose first language is one other than English. As I pointed out in Chapter 2, Dr. April Baker-Bell has written and spoken extensively about the ways in which many Black students' languages and literacies are considered both *less valid* and *less valuable* in the majority of school spaces. Of her time teaching English language arts in a Detroit-area high school at the start of her educational career, she writes:

> *As a speaker of Black Language myself, I recognized that my students were communicating in a language that was valid and necessary at home, in school, and in the hood, but I was receiving pressure from school administrators to get the students to use the "language of school." (2020, p. 4)*

At the time, Dr. Baker-Bell says,

> *I did not have the language to name the white linguistic hegemony that was embedded in our disciplinary discourses, pedagogical*

*practices and theories of language, nor did I have the tools to engage my students in critical conversations about Anti-Black Linguistic Racism. (p. 4)*

She goes on to define Anti-Black Linguistic Racism as "the linguistic violence, persecution, dehumanization, and marginalization that Black Language-speakers experience in schools and everyday life" (p. 11), a form of oppression that also dismisses and denies the rich linguistic rules and practices, derived from its ancestral "kinship" to a variety of West African languages (Kifano & Smith, 2003), that are embedded in Black Language (also commonly referred to as AAVE, or African American Vernacular English). This is evident in how children who speak Black Language (BL) are said to, for example, "omit" or "delete" sounds or entire words, implying that BL is a "lesser-than" or "simpler" version of White Mainstream English, the assumed "norm." As language scholars Subira Kifano and Ernie A. Smith argue:

> *Because Africologists view the language of African descendants as an African language system, [they] contend that in the sentences "You the man" and "That girl she nice" there has been no "deleted," "dropped," or "omitted" copula or verb "to be." As an African language system that has an equational or equative clause structure,* the verb "to be" never existed in the first place. *(pp. 81–82; my emphasis)*

### "Different" ≠ "Deficit"

While certainly race, culture, and ethnicity—and the social power assigned to these factors—influence how students' language and literacy practices are either privileged or viewed as a deficit in school spaces, socioeconomic class also often plays a role, as it so egregiously does in the discourse around the so-called word gap. As Althier M. Lazar, Patricia A. Edwards, and Gwendolyn Thompson McMillon (2012) point out in their book *Bridging Literacy and Equity: The Essential Guide to Social Equity Teaching*, while poverty *is* linked to underachievement on literacy assessment measures that inherently perpetuate dominant ideas around what kinds of literacy practices "count" in the world (which, as I have already argued in Chapter 1, disproportionately reflect an "autonomous" view of literacy), "it does not determine low literacy." The kinds of literacy practices valued in the homes and communities of children with low socioeconomic status "may look different" from those most valued in typical school spaces; however, these authors write, "*different* does not mean *deficit*": "

> Families living in poverty have been found to engage in rich and varied experiences with print and . . . these experiences tend to be embedded in families' everyday practices" (p. 20).

For example, the research of renowned linguistic anthropologist Shirley Brice Heath has demonstrated over and over again that the literate practices of what she has called "mainstream" (e.g., White, middle-class, English-speaking) communities often use the kinds of discourse patterns most often echoed in schools. (Recall that Dr. Baker-Bell also uses the term "mainstream" in order to "foreground the relationship between language, race, anti-Black racism, and white linguistic supremacy" [2020, p. 2]; here I am continuing to use the term alongside an acknowledgment that while linguistic and literacy patterns do exist, no community's practices are monolithic.) One such pattern is the "initiation–reply–evaluation" sequence, which is often heard during so-called mainstream families' bedtime story reading. In the first few years of life, Heath writes,

> the child [from the mainstream family] is socialized into [this particular sequence], repeatedly described as the central structural feature of classroom lessons. . . . Teachers ask their students questions which have answers prespecified in the mind of the teacher. Students respond, and teachers provide feedback, usually in the form of an evaluation. Training in this pattern begins very early in the labelling activities of mainstream parents and children. (1982, pp. 51–52)

In addition, children from a large number of White, middle-class families learn the "rules" of particular book-centered literacy events very quickly, which include norms around how and where to direct their attention, how to echo the structure of mainstream stories in their own "fictive narratives," and so on. "A pervasive pattern of all these features," Heath says, "is the authority which books and book-related activities have in the lives of both the preschoolers and members of their primary network" (p. 53):

> *By the time they enter school, [children from mainstream families] have had continuous experience as information-givers; they have learned how to perform in those interactions which surround literate sources throughout school . . . [and] have developed habits of performing which enable them to run through the hierarchy of preferred knowledge about a literate source and the appropriate sequence of skills to be displayed in showing knowledge of a subject. (p. 56)*

These "habits of performing" amount to a kind of "intellectual property" or capital that children who've learned them at home have unfairly earned even before entering formal schooling.

In contrast, in some communities, such as the working-class community that Heath studied, books are primarily used as *information receptacles*, offering children knowledge about topics like the alphabet, animals, and religion. While they may be questioned about the books they've read (or that have been read to them) by caregivers, these questions are most often the kind that probe for literal understandings or specific "recall"-type facts. As a result, Heath writes, "[these] children can handle successfully the initial stages of lessons. But when they move ahead to . . . activities considered more advanced and requiring more independence, they are stumped" (p. 63). In addition, their own composed stories often take the form of retellings of stories they already know, which, today, frequently reflects the films, television shows, and video games that children consume (and which, as I pointed out in Chapter 2, are often dismissed or devalued in most writing workshop classrooms).

## THE IRE/IRF SEQUENCE

The initiation–reply–evaluation (IRE), or feedback (IRF), sequence is a common structure in many classrooms in which large-group discussions are controlled by the teacher—often, but not always, using known-answer questions (see Chapter 2 for an explanation of these). An example of an IRF sequence would be something like,

**TEACHER:** What do we always start a sentence with? Maja?

**MAJA:** A capital letter.

**TEACHER:** Right. And where can we remind ourselves of what our capital letters are supposed to look like if we forget? Kendrick?

**KENDRICK:** Um . . . there [points to alphabet cards on wall].

**TEACHER:** Yes!

While there is nothing inherently wrong about this kind of sequence, the overreliance on this particular pedagogical tool can often inadvertently

- hamper students' developing skills around engaging in a variety of effective conversations;
- hinder the development of a democratic classroom, where students have an equitable chance at contributing their knowledge and/or asking pertinent questions; and
- perpetuate socially dominant ways of engaging in discussions (e.g., using controlled turn-taking) rather than embracing culturally diverse conversational methods.

For more on this, see "The Role of Conversation and Culture in the Systematic Design of Instruction" by Nancy P. Scheel and Robert C. Branch (1993). I also highly recommend Kara Pranikoff's (2017) book *Teaching Talk: A Practical Guide to Fostering Student Thinking and Conversation* as an accessible, engaging guide for educators interested in nurturing students' classroom talk in a way that is affirming of their diverse strengths.

Does this mean that the ways that children who do not come from so-called mainstream families participate in literacy events are less important—or "less than" as a whole—than the ways in which children from "mainstream" families do? Of course not. In fact, when Heath (1982) studied the literacy practices of children from a majority-Black community, for example, she found that the vast majority of them "already use narrative skills [e.g., creative, analogical storytelling] highly rewarded in the upper primary grades" (p. 72). She also found that the caregivers and other adults from this community continually contextualized the environments in which they and their children found themselves and frequently engaged in literacy events in community with others, synthesizing the meaning of texts "as a whole" rather than in isolation (p. 69). Heath's findings, which reflect the richness and complexity of the literacy and language practices of many socially non-dominant communities, are echoed in the research of a large number of other, more contemporary literacy scholars (Bellanger, 1997; T. T. Flores, 2018; Muhammad, 2012).

## Nurturing a Learning Environment That Values the Literacy and Language Practices of All Students

None of this is meant to imply that there are *never* reasons to be concerned about a student's literacy or language development, or that all attempts to "intervene" in order to provide a student what they need to successfully engage in school literacy practices are unreasonable, discriminatory, or oppressive. Rather, what I mean to communicate is how essential it is for educators to critically consider the ways in which we often frame certain students' literacy and language practices over others', particularly in light of the kinds of patterns that exist in terms of who is more likely to be either formally or informally deemed "struggling" or "in need of intervention" (see Chapter 1 for statistics).

Given our own socialization as literacy educators, and given that the majority of classroom spaces within the United States continue to reflect the dominant social identities of those whose literacy and language practices are most privileged in school spaces, how can we work toward a more anti-oppressive practice that (1) not just recognizes but honors the rich literacy and language practices of *all* our students, *and* (2) helps our students themselves recognize, critique, disrupt, and transcend dominant narratives around literacy?

One of the ways that we can do this, of course, is first by changing the lens through which we view students' literacy and language practices by embodying a culturally responsive teaching approach, which I referenced in Chapter 2 and which Dr. Geneva Gay defines as "using the cultural characteristics, experiences, and perspectives of ethnically diverse students as conduits for teaching them more effectively" (2002, p. 106). As Dr. Gay points out, part of this work includes making explicit and ongoing attempts to recognize, understand, and integrate into our pedagogy the ways in which different cultural and ethnic groups approach communication, learning, problem solving, and so on, as well as how they contribute to shared knowledges. This can be tricky, of course, when we recognize that many individuals identify with multiple cultural groups, that culture is both fluid and dynamic, and—again—that people are not monolithic. However, the more we commit to truly knowing and celebrating our students, decentering dominant knowledges and assumptions around what constitutes "literacy" and "appropriate" or "effective" language use, and broaden our ideas about how readers and writers interact with texts (as well as what itself *constitutes* a "text"), the closer we are to embracing and centering a diversity of literacy and language practices in our schools and classrooms.

It's worth pointing out, I think, that when considering the varying languages/language practices of children and their inclusion in school literacy spaces, many educators—as well as those outside of classrooms who enact the vast majority of language policies—more readily accept this inclusion when it is couched in the language of Reggio Emilia (an educational philosophy borne out of Northern Italy) and its embrace of the "hundred languages of children." They are less likely to do so, if my own experience is any indication, when faced with the varied language practices of Black, Brown, and Indigenous children. Why might that be the case?

## Knowing and Celebrating Our Students

It is not easy to truly "know" each and every student we teach; regardless, we *must* consider this an essential part of our work as educators.

When I was an English Teaching student at the University of New Hampshire, I was taught a simple exercise, attributed to the beloved literacy educator Donald Graves, that my instructor called "10 Things" and that I used often throughout my time as a classroom teacher. The idea behind the activity was not only to help us learn to gauge how well we knew (or didn't know) our students, but also to consider how well *they* knew *us*. The way it works is as follows:

- Using any piece of paper that's blank on one side, fold it in thirds in order to create three columns.
- In the left column, list each of your students' names from memory. (For those who teach a large number of students, it's highly recommended that you start with just one group or class.) Try not to use alphabetical order, class-roster order, or table groups to help you remember; just write the names down as they come to mind.
- In the middle column, jot one thing you know about each student that has nothing to do with school (Try to jot something positive or, at the very least, something neutral about that student— e.g., they enjoy skateboarding). In addition, make a note of how you've learned this bit of information.
- In the right column, put a check mark or a star if you're 100% sure that student knows you know this about them because—for example—you've talked about it with them.
- Keep doing this exercise every so often throughout the year until you can list 10 things you know about each student (and that they *know* you know).

No matter how often I do this exercise, I discover something new. For example, I can see, plain as day, which students come to my mind first, which helps me reflect on why that is. Is it because my perception is that they typically need a lot of academic or emotional support from me? Is it because I consider them class "leaders"? Or is it simply that our personalities just seem to complement each other, so we've interacted a lot more? I also, obviously, discover who *doesn't* come to mind as easily, which helps me set goals for how I might try to get to know them better. This activity also helps me reflect on how much I know about students' home lives or families, which is a crucial step toward recognizing their families' literacy and language practices—for if we don't know the spaces, places, and communities our students inhabit outside of school, how will we ever know what values, norms, and practices to acknowledge, celebrate, and center *in* school? In our curriculum and instructional practices?

Another approach to getting to know our students that I appreciate is one that educator and author Cornelius Minor writes about in his book *We Got This: Equity, Access, and the Quest to Be Who Our Students Need Us to Be* (2019). Minor reminds us that our "superpower" as educators is listening to our students—really *listening*:

> [A]uthentic listening and the actions that result from it [is] the most radical of all teacher behaviors. When we seek to craft better realities for our students . . . our listening has to be informed by what we know, by what we are learning, and by our desire to actually hear what [they] are telling us. (p. 15–16).

Minor offers his readers a glimpse into his own listening mind—visualized as a "mental matrix" of sorts (p. 22)—that goes beyond the previous activity by not only connecting what he is learning about his students to their peers (e.g., "Are there other kids [in my class] who like the same thing?"), but also by considering how he intends to use what he's learned about his students to inform his practice as an educator and ensure that his students feel safe, comfortable, and—above all—heard.

## Noticing and Naming What Students Can Do

A third way to get to know our students, particularly in regard to their literacy and language practices, is by building a habit of what I call "can-do" noticing. In other words, instead of perseverating on all of the things that our students *can't* do (yet), let's make it our job to notice, acknowledge, and celebrate what they *can* do as readers and writers—while also being transparent with them, and explicitly educating them, about the languages and literacies of power that exist in our society.

As the anti-oppressive literacy education framework makes clear, all students engage in literacy and language practices that are both valid and valuable. To push this notion further, I firmly believe—and have seen it illustrated throughout my career—that *all students know, have, or are able to do something* that would be useful to teach another reader or writer. One of the ways I center and make such knowledges, attitudes, and practices visible is by making student mentorship a vital part of my practice.

### "What Can We Learn From _____?"

This can, of course, look different depending on the grade level of the students. In Chapter 2, I briefly mentioned the ways in which my colleagues used writing groups to encourage their students to support one another through their composing processes. Working in grades K–6, I have frequently used charting to help highlight the ways my readers, writers, and speakers might inspire and support one another to use various craft techniques, processes, and problem-solving strategies. This practice is especially important for those students who are not typically called upon to share their brilliance with classmates, particularly those who've been identified as having a reading-, writing-, or speaking-based learning disability.

I often tell educators with whom I work the story of Reagan (pseudonym), who by many accounts was a "struggling" third grader the year I co-taught in her class. Impulsive, opinionated, and brutally honest, Reagan was often so distracted by what was going on around her—and by her own racing thoughts—that she was rarely celebrated in the classroom as someone whose knowledge and work were valued. However, when my colleague and I made it our habit to look for how each of our students could potentially mentor another student, we quickly recognized an important strength (among many!) of Reagan's. Reagan was hyper-self-aware and both knew and frequently advocated for what she needed. When it came time to write, a practice she enjoyed, she always asked my co-teacher and me if she could sit in a corner of the room—where she felt safe and cozy—and draw the shade on the window in that area of the room, further dampening any sensory stimulation that could potentially distract her.

We knew that Reagan's knack for both knowing and advocating for herself was something that many of her classmates could learn from. With her permission, we highlighted her as one of our student mentors and asked her to share with her classmates what she did to both *tune into her specific needs* and *communicate those needs*. While her mentorship at the time was not writing specific, Reagan openly shared some of the language she often used to advocate for herself, which we added to the chart as potential sentence stems. Soon, her influence spread to many of her classmates, who began to pay close attention to how the environment affected them when it came time for them to work independently and *used the language Reagan had taught them* to communicate their individual needs. As an added bonus, they began to explicitly support/advocate for one another as well.

This kind of charting/mentorship can also be employed when considering how to highlight the different ways in which our students engage in dialogue or debate (even during informal conversations, like morning meeting) and when collectively creating norms for whole- and small-group conversations. I can remember several students I've had over the years who struggled with completing any sort of written task, but who served as role models when it came time for classroom conversations. There was Isaac, a sixth grader, who often made sure to clarify what someone else had said in order to avoid making assumptions (e.g., "When you say _____, do you mean . . . "), and Gabriela, a kindergartener, who—after engaging in a class-wide, months-long inquiry around "interesting words" —rarely missed an opportunity to point one out during an interactive read aloud. Embodied literacies matter too; I'm thinking of Darius, who rarely verbalized his thinking during class-wide conversations but whose active meaning-making was apparent in his lively facial expressions. (When considering these kinds of literacy practices and potential student mentorship, it is important, as always, to acknowledge and disrupt our socialized assumptions around which practices are worthy of being noticed and named in this way.)

Building a habit of noticing and explicitly naming what students *can* do as readers, writers, and speakers—and how they can potentially serve as a mentor to others—is a seemingly simple, but incredibly powerful, shift that not only changes the entire lens with which we view our students and their varied language and literacy practices but changes how they view each other. In all of my years as an educator, I have developed few habits that have so substantially transformed my practice as a literacy educator like this one has.

## Knowing and Celebrating Students' Families

Beyond getting to know our students, it is equally important (and often much more challenging) to get to know our students' families and their literacy and language practices. More so, it is important to do this in ways that are culturally responsive. Numerous impediments to building mutually supportive relationships with families include a lack of trust between caregivers and school personnel, language differences (including unfamiliarity with educational "jargon"), a noninclusive environment, and general life demands on the part of both families and educators. In addition, educators, regardless of their racial or ethnic identities (but more so for White educators), often position themselves as being "saviors" of both their students and the families. Because this "savior complex" is so pervasive and harmful, it is something that many educators need to intentionally work to disrupt.

### THE COMPLEXITY OF THE "SAVIOR COMPLEX"

A savior complex is an (often subconscious) psychological need to feel as though one is "saving" someone else from their problems or circumstances. Educators in films and television (e.g., *Freedom Writers* [2007], *Dangerous Minds* [1995], etc.) are often depicted in a way that reflects a "White savior complex" (WSC), where the teacher, most often a White woman, is portrayed as determined to "fix" her (usually Black and Brown) students and/or their lives outside of school. In real life, we sometimes see the WSC rear its ugly, racist head when educators describe themselves as teaching in a "Title 1" or "urban" school, with "Title 1" and "urban" used as a performative code for "I teach Black and Brown students and therefore am a good person."

Alternatively, in her heavily critiqued but hugely influential essay entitled "The Silenced Dialogue: Power and Pedagogy in Educating Other

People's Children," Lisa Delpit (1988) warns that such a phenomenon can develop when power relations among educators, students, and students' caregivers go unnoticed or unacknowledged and can be especially pervasive even in self-described "liberal" or "progressive" educational spaces. In these spaces, she writes, "the primary goal" is not to "fix" students but instead "for children to become autonomous, to develop fully who they are in the classroom setting without having arbitrary, outside standards forced upon them" (p. 285). The problem with this particular type of savior mentality, she argues, occurs when this manifests in *not explicitly teaching students*, particularly Black and Brown students, *about* these standards—what they are, where (and from whom) their power comes from, and how we might ultimately work to change them. What this does, Delpit maintains, is set these students up for failure under the guise of "good intentions."

One of the first steps toward building positive relationships with families—and disrupting the savior mentality—is to interrogate our assumptions around a variety of social and cultural factors. These include:

- What constitutes a "family." Students are members of a wide variety of family structures that often include divorced, separated, unmarried, or undocumented parents, grandparents, and other extended-family members, and/or nonbiological caregivers. In addition, despite some progress toward recognizing families in which the heads of household are members of varying LGBTQIA+ communities, we still have a long way to go in terms of our assumptions and the language we use.
- What "family engagement" looks like. For some families, engagement looks like volunteering in the school or classroom, chaperoning a field trip, or purchasing much-needed supplies. For others, engagement might look like following class or school social media groups, offering to share a parent's or caregiver's knowledge about or expertise in something, or commenting on

a post on their child's digital portfolio. And some forms of family engagement may be even less visible to educators, particularly when there is less commonality around teachers' and family members' social and cultural identities.

- What kind of school-based knowledge or jargon is universally understood. Too often, we throw around phrases like "summative assessment," "balanced literacy," "science of reading," or "authentic audience" as if our students' families have a comprehensive understanding of what they mean—or how these things impact *their* child. And the acronyms—so many acronyms! Educators committed to an anti-oppressive practice recognize the importance of ensuring that we are using non-jargony language and/or checking for understanding without being patronizing.

As the sociologist and professor of education Sara Lawrence-Lightfoot (2003) writes in her book *The Essential Conversation: What Parents and Teachers Can Learn From Each Other*, the most effective teachers aim to build relationships with families "that are collaborative and authentic [and] that seek symmetry and alliance." These teachers, she says, "see parents as the first educators, are respectful of their experience and perspective, and listen carefully to their observations and insights" (p. 228).

We are much more likely to gather insight into their varied language and literacy practices through intentional invitations that are accessible, differentiated, and sensitive to a wide diversity of experiences. One such invitation is an exercise I first learned of through my colleague at the University of New Hampshire, Dr. Christina Ortmeier-Hooper (2013), who encourages her students to "map" their literacies alongside a variety of social and cultural influences (not unlike what scholar Deborah Brandt calls "sponsors" of literacy; i.e., the means through which "any agents . . . enable, support, teach, [or] model, as well as recruit, regulate, suppress, or withhold literacy—and gain advantage by it in some way" [1998, p. 166]). As part of this exercise, students are invited to consider questions like the following:

- Who are the individuals who have had an influence on your reading and writing life (both in and outside of school)?

- What groups of people have influenced your reading and writing life (both in and outside of school)?
- What spaces or places do you associate with literacy practices?
- What events have taken place in your life that have affected your literacy development, identity, or practice(s)?
- What artifacts or things have affected your development, identity, or practice as a reader/writer/speaker?

Each student is given a large composing space—for example, a piece of chart paper or poster board, in the center of which they write their name—and a collection of visual icons that loosely represent each of these kinds of influences. Students are then encouraged to write specifics on each icon (e.g., "Oma" or "Grammy" on one of the icons that represent an individual person), taping or gluing them on their map; the closer they place their icons to their name, the stronger an influence the identified element has had on their development, identity, and/or practice as a reader, writer, or speaker. After plenty of time to work on their own map, and depending on the level of trust and/or community that has been established within the class, students are then offered the opportunity to share their maps with a partner, a small group, and/or the whole group.

As Dr. Ortmeier-Hooper demonstrates in her 2013 book *The ELL Writer: Moving Beyond Basics in Secondary Schools*, this mapping activity can also serve as an opportunity for teachers to get to know their students on an ever-deeper level throughout the year, using the maps as a conferring tool through which periodic discussions about these elements—and students' decisions while composing their map, including the placement of each icon—might offer valuable insights into students' ideological perceptions around literacy and of their lives outside of school. Having said that, as Dr. Ortmeier and her colleagues Mario Ivo Lopes Fernandes and Alicia Clark-Barnes remind us in a chapter they wrote called "Units of Exchange: How Teachers Develop Assignments with Academic Currency for Plurilingual Identities" (2022), for multilingual students in particular, the labor involved in such identity-focused work must not only be explicitly acknowledged, but "should be translated into academic capital" (p. 78)—in other words, compensated through credit, grades, and other material benefits.

## Decentering Dominant Ideologies and Assumptions About Literacy and Language

In their 2017 chapter that I referenced earlier, Rosa and Flores encourage educators to examine what they call our "White listening subjectivities," which are not (contrary to popular belief) exclusive to White folks but which, instead, are embedded in our *collective* consciousness as a result of how we've been socialized as members of a racialized society. "The White speaking and listening subject," they argue, "should be understood not as a biographical individual but rather as an *ideological position*. . . . Thus, it is crucial to analyze the ways that a range of actors and entities privilege hegemonic Whiteness as it pertains to language and other social practices" (p. 177; my emphasis). For us as individuals, this positioning is not the result of an inherent desire within educators to oppress those whose language and literacy practices do not match our own (and/or those we perceive to have the most power); rather, it is a result of the barrage of explicit and implicit messages about language we've received since before we were even born.

To combat this, we must identify *where linguistic supremacy "hides" within our consciousness*—and by extension, within our policies, practices, media, and attitudes—and work both intentionally and collectively to acknowledge, disrupt, and resist it. Some of the questions we might ask ourselves, and encourage our students to ask, include:

- How are students whose first language is one other than English identified in our school/district? How are students whose first language is English but who can also speak/read/write another language referred to? How are the students in one or the other groups typically perceived? What are the similarities and differences?

- What "stories" do such identification labels—and the recognition of which students get which labels—tell about *whose linguistic and literacy practices* need to change in order for all students to reach their potential as learners in school spaces?
- What is the assumed "audience" of the compositions that students create? How does this affect the ways in which their work is typically assessed and evaluated?

## Decentering and Recentering

Beyond *decentering* dominant (e.g., White, Eurocentric) ideologies around literacy and language, we must also, as Drs. Carla España and Luz Yadira Herrera (2020) argue, "*re*center" emergent bilinguals' knowledges and practices (although—to be clear—their focus in the work I am citing here specifically revolves around the voices and experiences of bilingual Latinx students). "If we want to provide learning experiences that will help bilingual Latinx children to thrive," they write, "we must construct an educational narrative that places the lives and experiences of these children at the forefront of curriculum design and implementation" (p. 17). They offer a range of lessons in their book that support this work through practices like encouraging students to write using their entire repertoire of language practices (i.e., engage in translanguaging), using texts that reflect fluid language practices, and inviting students to create "counter-narratives" (p. 102) to those most often told through the stories and the histories we typically center in school.

In addition to creating counternarratives around language practices, we must create counternarratives around literacy in general that help decenter historically approved practices of power and privilege and that broaden our collective ideas about how readers and writers should (and do) interact with texts. This is work we will dig deeper into in Chapter 5.

## TRANSLANGUAGING

Translanguaging is a process and a pedagogical approach that rejects linguistically oppressive "borders" between languages and invites and encourages learners to choose which language (or combination of languages) they wish to use in order to compose a text and/or demonstrate their knowledge about a subject. Educators can also use translanguaging practices during their instruction and in the process of designing their classroom environment.

## Teaching in School Spaces That Are Predominantly White

OK: real talk. You may be reading this chapter and thinking,

- "But I teach in a school whose students all speak English!" *and/or*
- "All of my students are White!" *and/or*
- "But we don't have a lot of literacy and language variation at my school!"

To that I say, *Everything you have read in this chapter still applies.* Even when teaching children who are native English speakers, or whose home literacies match those that are afforded the most power in school spaces, we must work to decenter dominant narratives around whose literary and language practices are considered "appropriate" or the "norm." (Revisit the anecdote I told at the start of Chapter 3 if you don't believe me.) There are two reasons for this:

- One, our children are growing up in a society that is becoming ever more diverse—in *all* ways—and must develop strategies for negotiating a world that increasingly represents and reflects a wide range of racial, ethnic, linguistic, and cultural knowledges, stories, and lived experiences. We are doing our students a disservice by continuing to perpetuate oppressive ideas around whose language and literacy practices matter most.
- Two, it is important that we help *all* our students develop the critical consciousness and the language necessary to disrupt and dismantle oppressive literacy and language ideologies. *This is not*

*a matter of "indoctrinating" children into believing that their own language and literacy practices are "wrong" or inherently "oppressive";* rather, it's a matter of disrupting the—often invisible, but nevertheless pervasive—indoctrination that has taken place in educational spaces for centuries.

In fact, I would argue that if we ourselves hold a number of dominant identities and/or teach a majority of children who do, we have an *even greater obligation* to engage in the kinds of work outlined in this chapter. I offer even more suggestions for doing so below.

## Internal Work

- Reflect: How, if at all, have your ideas about students' differing literacy and language practices changed or shifted after reading this particular chapter? What are some things you are now aware of that you may not have noticed before? What are some things you think that *I*, as a White native English speaker, might be missing?
- Make a list of your professional literacy "mentors"—those to whom you have traditionally turned when looking for professional learning around literacy and language. (It would be even more powerful to google their photos and line them all up on the same document.) What do you notice about your professional "ancestry"? How representative of a wide variety of identities is your list?
  - In this book, I have intentionally cited the scholarship and ideas of folks who represent a wide range of identities. Who among those I've (so far) cited do you want to learn more from?

## External Work

- Choose *one* of the practices or strategies I offered for getting to know our students and/or their families in this chapter. If you can, partner with a trusted colleague to engage in the work together, even if only for planning purposes. Reflect on what you are learning about your students and their diverse literacy and language practices. How might you more effectively center these in your instructional practice? In your curriculum? In the learning environment as a whole?

- Continue to jot what you are noticing about where literacy oppression "lives" in your district/school/classroom using the table from Chapter 1 as a guide. Begin to consider where you and your colleagues might first begin to disrupt this oppression. Where might you have the most influence or professional "pull"? Who can you identify as a possible co-conspirator with whom you might collaborate around this?

# CHAPTER 5

# Meaning-Making Occurs Within a Variety of Equally Valid Communicative Channels or Modes

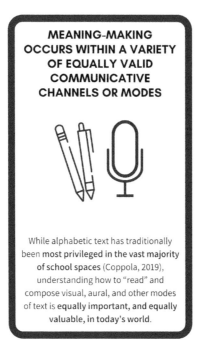

**MEANING-MAKING OCCURS WITHIN A VARIETY OF EQUALLY VALID COMMUNICATIVE CHANNELS OR MODES**

While alphabetic text has traditionally been **most privileged in the vast majority** of school spaces (Coppola, 2019), understanding how to "read" and compose visual, aural, and other modes of text is **equally important, and equally valuable, in today's world**.

*By being offered only one version of literacy, students are in effect denied literacy.*

> —Maisha T. Winn and Nadia Behizadeh (2011), "The Right to Be Literate: Literacy, Education, and the School-to-Prison Pipeline"

DOI: 10.4324/9781032658964-5

For decades, literacy educators and researchers have attempted to shift the balance around what kinds of communicative modes are privileged in schools and classrooms (Cope & Kalantzis, 2015; Kress & van Leeuwen, 2001; New London Group, 1996; Palmeri, 2012; Stockman, 2020). Recognizing the ubiquity of "alternative" or multimodal texts (and text-*making*) in the everyday lives of the vast majority of American children, youth, and adults, they have sought to provide justification for decentering monomodal (e.g., traditionally alphabetic) literacy practices in the educational lives of our students and—alongside hundreds of colleagues—offered a multitude of suggestions for ways this can be implemented in school learning spaces in ways both large and small.

## The Preponderance of Print

Despite this, the resilience of print-heavy forms of text in educational spaces has proved to be as strong as the dominance of the Western, White culture that sustains it. This is not to say, of course, that print literacy is privileged by *only* Western, White communities. This is also not to say that printed texts are inherently bad or are not useful; in fact, knowing how the growing accessibility of print text over time has made it possible, in many ways, to democratize knowledge, it would be foolish (and woefully inaccurate) to argue otherwise. However, as some historians have argued (and as I explore in some depth in Chapter 6), the dominance of print texts in society, and therefore in most schools and classrooms, has oftentimes served as a way for those with a disproportionate amount of social and political capital to determine the "acceptability" of individuals' levels of literacy—and consequently, in many cases, their very *personhood*. In her book *The Violence of Literacy*, J. Elspeth Stuckey (1991) specifically implicates literacy educators in this phenomenon and equates the teaching of print-literacy development with the teaching of products, or "artifacts":

> *The profession has an interest in believing in the enigmatic power of the literate artifact—a sort of homage to the solid demonstration of the result of literacy: the script, the printed page, the preserved manuscript, the student's five-paragraph essay. (p. 36)*

This interest, she argues throughout her book, boils down to the assurance of "the maintenance of white middle class values" (p. 122) through literacy—specifically, *print* literacy—itself.

## WORSHIP OF THE WRITTEN WORD

In 1999, equity and racial justice advocate Tema Okun wrote a piece called "White Supremacy Culture" which listed 15 characteristics of White supremacy she has found that many organizations "unconsciously use . . . as their norms and standards [that] make it difficult, if not impossible, to open the door to other cultural norms and standards" (p. 7). While the characteristics she listed were said to have been built upon the work of such racial justice and equity mentors as Dr. Beverly Daniel Tatum, Kenneth Jones, and others, she has also maintained that they were conceived of as a result of her own experiences as a consultant.

One of these characteristics, "Worship of the Written Word," describes the cultural habit of "honoring only what is written and only what is written to a narrow standard, even when what is written is full of misinformation and lies." Worship of the written word, Okun says, "includes erasure of *the wide range of ways we communicate with each other* and all living things" (my emphasis). Of the 11 antidotes to this prevailing characteristic are two that she developed alongside her colleague Cristina Rivera Chapman of the Earthseed Land Collective: (1) "dedicate time to practicing and honoring other ways of knowing and expression" and (2) "practice listening" in order to aid us in "remembering how to hold a spoken word with weight (without having to write it down)" (Okun, n.d.).

Sociolinguist Jenny Cook-Gumperz and her colleague, discourse analyst Deborah Keller-Cohen (1993), have also written about the ways that, throughout much of our history, print literacy has been accorded a certain status or privilege by those in power, particularly when it is positioned on a (false) binary opposite oral literacy practices. In their piece "Alternative Literacies in School and Beyond: Multiple Literacies of Speaking and Writing," they write:

> *The moment-to-moment production of talk has always had a different intellectual status from the products of pen and printing press. Any traditional definition of literacy has stressed the essential difference that occurs when ideas generated in talk are transposed or reconstituted in written form. (p. 283)*

"Written language," they argue, "is solidified by institutional arrangements of social relations necessary for its production" (p. 283), and an individual's ability to "control" this—that is, to adhere to sanctioned notions around "proper" English language use through the production of written text—"became the approved evidence of a literate person" (p. 284).

Sounds familiar, doesn't it?

When print and oral literacies are positioned as a dichotomy, we erase how heavily reliant print literacy is on oral language—as well as how exposure to print texts positively affects individuals' oral language development, including their vocabulary development.

### Resistance to Multimodal Texts

For someone like me, who has accrued a significant amount of social and professional capital via the creation of print "artifacts" that, for the most part, adhere to these sanctioned standards—the text you currently hold in your hands included!—these are uncomfortable ideas to grapple with. However, I also think a lot about how I was socialized to value alphabetic-heavy texts over other texts in school spaces, despite the fact that, outside of school, my reading and writing life included an enormous number of multimodal texts in the form of magazines, comics, catalogs, and illustrated stories, which has continued into my adulthood. In my 2019 book *Writing, Redefined: Broadening Our Ideas of What It Means to Compose*, around which much of this particular anti-oppressive principle is based, I write,

> *My obsession [with multimodal texts] continues to this day. In fact, few things make me happier than fishing out the latest New Yorker or Atlantic peeking its glossy little self out among the onslaught of bills, flyers, and bank statements piled up in my mailbox. I've even managed to project my undying love for magazines onto my long-suffering children, who've been gifted with everything from Highlights to American Girl to Teen Beat practically since they were old enough to eat solid foods. (p. 54)*

In spite of my personal affection for texts that incorporate more than one mode—which include texts like podcasts, TikTok videos, and digital stories, like those featured in online forums like the *New York Times*, *Autostraddle*, and *The Cut*, my pedagogy during the first several years that I worked as an ELA teacher rarely reflected this. The following is just one example.

It was the early 2000s, and I was teaching students in grades 6–8. At the time, there were few graphic novels written for middle school audiences that were available on the market; even so, I can remember that I'd had a number of students who devoured the books from Jeff Smith's *Bone* series, which was perpetually "on hold" at our school library. Reader, I'm not going to lie— I was *entirely perplexed* by the popularity of these books. Again, I loved reading comics and other multimodal texts as a kid—but *outside* of school! In school, I dutifully read my chapter books (even if those books *were* of the *Sweet Valley High* variety).

Unlike what continues to happen in many K–12 classrooms—and even some school libraries, such as the "soft censorship" tactic of temporarily removing comics and graphic novels from circulation (Hawkins, 2022)—I never explicitly prohibited my students from reading these multimodal texts. However, I do recall worrying that those who read them voraciously would "fall behind" because—well, because that wasn't *real* reading. Real reading—or rather, that which was sanctioned in school spaces—was the kind that was strictly alphabetic in nature.

## The Complexity of Multimodal Texts

But then, one day—my curiosity decidedly piqued—I read *Owly*. Do you know it? If not, *Owly* is a graphic novel series that first dropped in 2004 and is centered around a sweet, wide-eyed owl and his adventurous friends. There are few actual words in the *Owly* books; rather, author-illustrator Andy Runton relies on illustration and *emanata*—symbols that demonstrate a character's emotion, like exclamation points, tear drops, and bursts—to tell the story. I don't recall what compelled me to pick them up the first time, but oh—when I tell you how challenging it was for me to *read* those books! (This, despite the decades-long misconception that we only "learn to read" until third grade, after which we "read to learn.") I can still remember the visceral feeling of struggling to wrap my brain around what was happening. As a self-identified lifelong reader, I was humbled to realize how much skill it took to read contemporary graphic novels, which were far more sophisticated than the *Archie* and *Mad* magazine comics I'd hoarded two decades earlier. The way I viewed the practice of reading comics and graphic novels, and how much I valued that practice, was forever changed.

A note for those who are unfamiliar: All graphic novels are technically comics, which are traditionally defined as texts that feature *sequential visual artwork*. The term "graphic novel" did not actually enter the popular American lexicon until the late 1980s, after the publication in 1986 of both Alan Moore and Dave Gibbons's *Watchmen* and a collected volume of Art Spiegelman's nonfiction series *Maus*.

Unfortunately, I had already likely done harm to my students for years—particularly those who I mistakenly considered "reluctant" or "struggling" readers—by implicitly valuing a certain type of reading over another, equally valid, type. Again, this is not singular to my own personal experience or pedagogical practice. In a 2020 piece about comics and graphic novels for the *Washington Post*, Karen MacPherson, a librarian in Takoma Park, Maryland, wrote that "adult resistance to comics isn't unusual" and that "dealing with parents and teachers who see comics . . . as a low form of entertainment—instead of a valuable literacy tool—is a key topic of discussion among many children's librarians" (para. 3). Echoing the sentiments of those who have resisted the allure of comics for nearly a century, many educators consider these multimodal texts to be a less sophisticated, less complex form than more alphabetic-heavy texts, like chapter books and long-form expository pieces such as those featured in newspapers or magazines, despite numerous studies pointing to their complexity (Kelly & Kachorsky, 2022; Smith & Pole, 2018; Smith et al., 2017). But educators and caregivers are not the only ones to blame: As associate professor and former high school English teacher Sean Connors (2010) has pointed out, some *students* also "[question] the propriety of teaching graphic novels, particularly as a form of literature," which they sometimes assume "preclude[s] critical thinking" (p. 68). (It's worth noting, however, that since the publication of Dr. Connors's piece, graphic novels have exploded even further in popularity and have even been granted their own *New York Times* bestseller category, which was discontinued for three years but reinstated in the fall of 2019.)

## COMICS: THE UNLIKELY(?) SCAPEGOAT

For almost as long as comics have been around, they have been deemed by some to be the reason for the decline of our nation's youth (and their literacy practices).* Having long been a textual space through which to practice subversion and explore themes not often accessible in more mainstream kinds of texts, their popularity came to a head in the late 1940s when German-born psychiatrist Dr. Fredric Wertham wrote a series of scathing pieces (one in a popular women's magazine) declaring that comics were responsible for the post-WWII rise in "juvenile delin-quency" (Pyle & Cunningham, 2014) and that they were to blame for American youths' lack of reading proficiency (sound familiar?).

In response, comics were summarily seized from newsstands, declared to be unfit reading for those in the military, and burned by members of churches, schools, and even several Boy Scouts of America troops. In 1954, after a series of U.S. Senate hearings that equated the rise of comics with that of Communism, Judge Charles F. Murphy, the so-called Comics Czar, was hired to "clean up" the comic-book industry through the development and enforcement of the standards of the 1954 Comics Code Authority, which Murphy promised would ensure that "only good, clean, wholesome comic books will reach" America's homes (Price, 2019). The authority and its famous "Seal of Approval" was eventually phased out, with the last two major comics publishers finally dropping the seal in 2011 (Nyberg, n.d.).

*Interestingly, the moral panic over novel reading in England during the late 18th century involved similar claims about the decline of the populace—particularly of women! This quote from Ana Vogrinčič's arti-cle "The Novel-Reading Panic in 18th Century in England: An Outline of an Early Moral Media Panic" (2008) stands out in particular: "Novels were blamed for a motley range of evil, as summarized by Knox: 'If it be true that the present age is more corrupt than the preceding, the great multiplication of novels has probably contributed to its degener-acy' (Knox, 1778 in I. Williams, 1970: 304)" (p. 118).

## Evidence in Favor of Using Multimodal Texts in the Classroom

Regardless of such (mis)perceptions, there is a mountain of evidence that demonstrates the effectiveness of using comics in the classroom in a multitude of ways. In my own classroom practice, a number of students who I unfairly painted as "reluctant" readers and/or writers became decidedly *non*-reluctant when engaged in organic, student-led inquiries around how to compose comics and graphic novels (which also, by design, taught these and other students how to effectively *read* them). In classrooms in which I served as a coach or support specialist, I experienced firsthand the ways that students who had been identified with a language-based learning disability positively shined when encouraged to experiment with the writing of these forms of composition during writers' workshop, often serving as writing mentors to their nondisabled classmates.

## Emergent Bilinguals

In addition, a number of studies with emergent bilingual children and youth have pointed to the benefits of using comics and other multimodal texts (e.g., picture books) in order to both activate and build their background knowledge as well as to increase the English vocabulary necessary for the effective reading of more print-heavy texts (Clark, 2017). This is not only due to the internal motivation that many children and youth naturally have to read these often visually engaging texts; it is also due to many of the linguistic features embedded in these forms—for example, speech bubbles, special lettering, and captions—that help scaffold the reader's ability to make meaning. Furthermore, as Pacheko and Smith (2015) found in their study of the multimodal compositional practices (or "multimodal codemeshing") of bilingual adolescents in an urban school, such practices "offered students of varying degrees of proficiency in English and their heritage language the opportunity to communicate messages to multiple audiences, convey multidimensional and nuanced meanings, and give voice to often unheard voices in the classroom" (p. 308).

I don't necessarily feel like I have to say this, but just in case: Friendly reminder that many picture books are extraordinary pieces of literature and are appropriate, useful, and engaging for students of any age.

## Immigrant Children and Youth

In working with immigrant and refugee students, many educators—among them Thi Bui, a teacher at Oakland International High School; Nora Litz, a Philadelphia-based Mexican American activist/artist; and Michael Bitz of the New York City–based Comic Book Project—have found that comics, like other forms of art, can help children and youth whose first language is one other than English make critical connections between and among their various communities and safely process their (sometimes traumatic) life experiences. Not only that, but such a visually heavy form of text can often serve as a "bridge" to learning about and developing important interpersonal connections with these students when an educator's or a student's first language can sometimes pose a linguistic barrier to the development of positive relationships. Of an invitation she offers to her ninth- and 10th-grade students to tell their immigration stories in the form of a comic, Thi Bui writes:

> When I began teaching at Oakland International High School, I had lofty ideas about world events and issues I would be able to discuss with such an international mix of students. I too am an immigrant; I left Vietnam as a refugee when I was a child. But what I quickly realized stood between us was a language gap wider than any ocean. My pseudo-command of three other languages didn't even begin to cover the multitude of languages that my students spoke.

She continues:

> The comics project began as a way for me to better understand my students. I found that if I taught everyone a new language, governed by a few simple conventions like panels and speech balloons, then we would have a common way of communicating that allowed students to surprise me. Over the years, as I learned to ask them better questions, my students have surprised, informed, inspired, and moved me to tears with their stories. (2012)

## Beyond Comics and Graphic Novels

In my work with K–12 literacy teachers across the country, not only have I observed the same resistance to using comics and graphic novels (beyond the occasional "mini" unit or end-of-the-year "treat") that I wrote about earlier; I've observed a similar dearth of invitations for students to read, compose, and/or analyze multimodal (or "alternative") texts in *any* form. Dr. David E. Kirkland (2004), Distinguished Professor of English and Urban Education at New York University, has pointed this out as well, arguing that not only have writing teachers been, and continue to be, disproportionately White but also that "many of them affirm almost completely traditional writing pedagogies that accentuate [W]estern thought and ideology" (p. 83). While the most common reason for focusing almost exclusively on alphabetic texts cited by the literacy educators I've worked with is the preponderance of these texts on high-stakes standardized assessments—and therefore, the need to "prepare" students for such assessments—other recurrent reasons include a perceived "unfamiliarity" with multimodal texts, a lack of knowledge around how to assess students' multimodal literacy practices, and a concern that too much of an emphasis on these texts would leave students "behind" in their reading/writing development.

Considering the dominance of exclusively alphabetic texts within most standardized assessments, and the pressure we feel to teach our way out of the perpetual literacy "crisis," these reasons are not—well, *unreasonable*. However, as experts within our field, it is our responsibility to use our professional and political capital to advocate for changes that would help ensure that our pedagogy is more relevant to students' everyday, multitextual lives as well as more inclusive of a wide variety of lived experiences and literacy practices, past and present. This is true across the board, regardless of our students' identities and/or perceived abilities—but it is *especially true* when we acknowledge that the students most affected by our continued overprivileging of print text are those who are traditionally the most underserved by dominant school literacy practices. This includes, of course, students whose home and/or cultural literacy practices do not reflect those most often taught in school.

Kate T. Anderson and Dani Kachorsky offer some excellent recommendations for effectively assessing students' multimodal compositions
in the 2019 piece they wrote for the journal *English Teaching Practice &
Critique* called "Assessing Students' Multimodal Compositions: An Analysis of the Literature."

For example, in writing about the "contested histories" of Indigenous
peoples as a result of Western colonization, which included attempting
to "civilize" Indigenous folks through Eurocentric notions around literacy, Linda Tuhiwai Smith (2008) contends that

> *the idea of contested stories and multiple discourses about the past,
> by different communities . . . is very much a part of the fabric of
> communities that value oral ways of knowing [my emphasis]: These
> contested accounts are stored within genealogies, within the land-
> scape, within weavings and carvings, even within the personal
> names that many people carried. The means by which these histories
> were stored was through their systems of knowledge. (p. 33)*

However, these particular "systems of knowledge"—and the practices
within them that help us make meaning of our world—are rarely present, or even acknowledged, in K–12 literacy spaces.

Additionally, as Naa Dede Awula Addy (2018) points out in her
dissertation examining the socioculturally influenced literacy practices of individuals, and specifically the early language and literacy
practices of Black middle-class families in the southeastern United
States, many literacy and language scholars (Shirley Brice Heath,
Geneva Smitherman, Victoria Purcell-Gates, etc.) have identified a
number of home literacy practices that tend to be stratified along
racial and/or class lines. For example, the preponderance of "book-
like" talk or an emphasis on exclusively print-based story narratives are
more commonly observed in White communities, particularly those
that are characterized as being middle to upper class. In addition,
Addy writes,

*When it comes to stories, Heath's (1983) research suggests that within black communities, stories are conceptualized more as oral accounts that are jointly created rather than as narratives written within books. She argues that stories are also meant to be fictionalized and elaborated, rather than necessarily representing a literal representation of reality. This approach to narrative contrasts with how narratives are typically framed in white communities, in which more emphasis is placed on accuracy and factuality. (p. 4)*

Drs. Detra Price-Dennis, Gholdy Muhammad, Valerie Kinloch, Delicia Tiera Greene, and Marcelle Haddix, as well as many other scholars, have also written extensively about the ways in which they have specifically observed African American girls using multimodal forms, alongside digital media, to "make visible" their academic knowledge when, too often, such knowledge is marginalized or dismissed in school spaces. In "Developing Curriculum to Support Black Girls' Literacies in Digital Spaces," for example, Dr. Price-Dennis (2016) writes that "in essence, Black girls' literacies are multimodal and embody a critical stance that fosters dexterity across genres, platforms, audiences, and registers" (p. 340). And in the May 2022 issue of *The Language and literacy Spectrum*, Dr. Greene describes a self-designed qualitative study centered around her Adolescent Literacies and Multimodalities course, the result of which reminds us that, combined, multimodal and digital literacies "serve as counternarratives and are emancipatory in nature providing Black girls the freedom, creative control, autonomy, and agency to author their lives" (para. 1). "Cultivating multimodal pedagogies for Black girls is dire," Greene argues, in order to "allow Black girls to (re)tell their stories" that, far too often within school spaces, position them at the center of a deficit narrative (para. 50–52).

## Critical Multimodal Literacy

Using multimodality to adopt a critical stance embodies what Cappello et al. (2019) have termed "critical multimodal literacy," a framework that they argue "describes the ways that children use multimodal tools such as sketches, photographs, drama, or songs for personal meaning-making, critique, and agentive learning in classrooms" (p. 209). In particular, they contend that employing such a framework "opens up equitable learning opportunities" for children and youth whose literacies and ways of making meaning are traditionally marginalized.

Their framework consists of four dimensions:

1. Communicating and Learning with Multimodal Tools, which "[provide] possibilities beyond the printed form" (p. 209);
2. Restorying, Representing, and Redesigning, which invites students, essentially, to reclaim "their own identities, roles, and trajectories within the dominant narratives circulating within schooling and other societal institutions" (p. 210);
3. Acknowledging and Shifting Power Relationships, which they argue can happen "when children incorporate their perspectives and knowledge about racial, cultural, and linguistic diversity into composing processes," resulting in a potential shift in traditional teacher-student dynamics (p. 211); and
4. Leveraging Multimodal Resources to Critique and Transform Sociopolitical Realities (p. 212), such as was demonstrated when the fifth-grade students with whom my colleague Kitri Schaefer and I worked in the spring of 2021 used infographics and digital narratives to share what they learned about food, water, and/or environmental justice in order to urge their audience to advocate for systemic changes within these social sectors.

Sharing the research and collegial expertise that I've curated here is *not* to say, of course, that communities based on race, culture, Indigeneity, class, or other social identities are uniform, or that one community's literacy practices are more or less valid than another's. (If you've been paying attention up until now, you know that I am actually arguing quite the opposite!) Rather, it's to point out, once again, how most school-sanctioned literacy practices, including the emphasis on print literacy practices over those that are oral, visual, gestural, or multimodal in nature, disproportionately favor those that most often tend to exist—and have historically existed—in White, middle-class communities, and that the process of making meaning can (and does!) happen through a wide variety of equally valid modes.

## MODES, FORMS, GENRES, AND MEDIA

The differences between a "mode" and a "form" and a "genre" can be confusing, and when we include discussions around "media," well—our brains can turn to mush. While there is no definitive consensus around these concepts, I find that it's useful to explain them in this way:

Mode: This involves decisions about how an author has attempted to communicate (or during the act of writing, *intends to communicate*) meaning. Examples: alphabetic, visual, aural, gestural, spatial, and so forth.

Form: The form of a composition is determined by how it is organized or structured (form = format). The most common form taught in school spaces, by far, is the essay form. Other forms of composition include short stories, infographics, song lyrics, comics, and poetry (which, itself, can take on a variety of different forms).

Genre: The genre of a text is determined by its content or tone, although technique and length are also sometimes used as factors. Fiction and nonfiction are the two major genres, but some subgenres include fantasy, true crime, humor, and science fiction.

Medium: The materials and tools *through which* meaning is "delivered" are what constitute the kind of media one uses or has used. For example, this might look like the kind of paint (e.g., gouache or watercolor) someone has chosen to use. In other kinds of spaces someone might choose to use pen and paper, their own body, and/or a digital tool such as a slide presentation to deliver their meaning.

## Incorporating Multimodality Into Our Practice

Shifting our pedagogical practice to include more opportunities for students to read, compose, and even perform texts that encompass a wide variety of modes is not so much an instructional choice but an ethical imperative. In her exploration of immigrant students' use of "multiple representational resources . . . across virtual and material spaces," Wan Shun Eva Lam (2006) points out that "the nature of work and leisure in post-industrial economies is increasingly centered around the production and consumption of 'texts' in various forms, including oral language, visual and graphical representations, audio records, print documents, and digital and online communications" and argues that "literacy pedagogy needs to *move beyond* its largely rule-based, monolingual, and monocultural framework that is centred around the nation state" (pp. 174–175; my emphasis). But how to do that in a system that was, in many ways, *built* upon the idea of preserving the literacy and language practices of a protected class of people?

### Multimodal Affordances

One step toward decentering exclusively alphabetic modes of representing and making meaning in our instructional practice is by exploring, and inviting our students to explore, the *affordances*, or the potentialities and the constraints, of different modes. In other words, what does the visual mode "afford us" as meaning-makers that the alphabetic/print mode does not? How do these affordances change when they are combined through a form like a comic, an infographic, or a picture book? How do they change even further when read or created through a different medium—for example, a digital comic versus a comic printed on paper?

### THE KINESTHETIC-TACTILE MODE

Incorporating the kinesthetic-tactile mode is also worth exploring with readers and writers of all ages, particularly as it relates to the reading and writing experiences of students with visual impairments and other physical and/or learning disabilities. Colorado's Build a Better Book (BBB) program serves as an excellent model for engaging children and youth in the design of inclusive, multimodal texts (https://www .colorado.edu/project/bbb/). Using tactile materials or "loose parts"— for example, buttons, seeds, and yarn—throughout the composition process also builds upon the work of Reggio Emilia–inspired educators, who embrace the concept of teaching and learning "in a world no longer bonded by a printed text only" (Miller & McVee, 2012, p. 1).

For example, consider the various forms of a popular text like Christina Soontornvat's (2020) award-winning middle-grade fantasy novel *A Wish in the Dark*. What does the audio version (narrated by actor-director Greta Jung) afford listeners of the book that the print version does not, and vice versa? What is *enhanced* or, perhaps, *lost* when students view the book's trailer (https://youtu.be/Wvmbba8-nxM), which incorporates both visual images and music? How might these affordances help us and our students make intentional decisions when choosing a text to read or when composing a text? Another excellent resource to use to explore the idea of affordances is Gavin Aung Than's Zen Pencil comics, which are inspirational quotes and speeches that Gavin, a *New York Times*–bestselling cartoonist, adapted or "remixed" as comic stories between the years 2012 and 2018 (https://www.zenpencils.com/). How does the process of meaning-making—and/or the experience of the reader as a whole—change when reading or listening to these quotes in their original print- or audio-based forms versus reading Than's comic version? Exploring the different affordances of a particular mode can also open up important conversations about text accessibility, such as how to create effective alt-text or adaptable comics for blind and low-vision readers or why it is so important to use the caption feature when creating a TikTok.

## Remixing

Another invitation that can encourage explorations around alternative modes of text in the classroom is to have students *remix* a text—one that either they or someone else has created. A remix is something that has been revised or altered from its original iteration that offers audiences a new "take" or experience (e.g., a cover version of a popular song). In the literacy classroom, this can take the form of inviting students to select a piece of writing they have already composed—a story, a poem, an informational text—and consider re-"writing" it using a different modality (or a combination of modalities). For example, students could turn an informational essay they've written into an infographic or a short informational video using tools like Canva, Animoto, or Loom. Alternatively, they could be invited to select an excerpt from a favorite text, such as a particular scene in a novel, and turn it into something new: a comic, or an audio reading, or an embodied performance. Part of any invitation to remix a text should include an opportunity for learners to reflect upon and/or discuss how using different modes of composition changes the compositional process—as well as the reading of the new, remixed text.

## EMBODIED LITERACIES

In her book *Embodied Literacies: Imageword and a Poetics of Teaching*, Kristie S. Fleckenstein (2003) urges educators to "disestablish our definitions of literacy as dominantly and aggressively linguistic" and to "seek an alternative imaginary" that enables us to broaden our view of literacy as including "more than words, more than language" (p. 2). "By failing to attend to imagery," she writes—imagery that surrounds us on every level, in seemingly every space—"we cannot address how our images imprison and free us, how they hurt and heal us, and how they oppress and transform us" (p. 4).

Within this concept of "embodied literacies" are considerations around how we (and our students) conduct and express meaning through our bodies. For example, in her chapter "Reader Response and Embodied Performance," Grace Enriquez (2015) writes about the many ways in which children and youth compose what she calls "body-poems" within the classroom that arise from their "critical transactions with texts."

She critiques how the normative surveillance of students' body-poems can play out in school spaces (especially when students' body-poems do not conform to "normative" assumptions about how readers should respond to texts) and suggests the many ways in which educators might conceive of these poems as meaningful information that can be used to understand student responses to texts and how they reflect these students' identities as readers.

I include the concept of "embodied literacies" here because I find the concepts of "imageword" and "body as text" equally fascinating and consider them to be enormously relevant to the particular framework principle that this chapter focuses on.

## Multimodal Counternarratives

Engaging students in such a practice opens up possibilities for them to seek out and create counternarratives, an important consideration for educators seeking to develop an anti-oppressive literacy pedagogy. In fact, while the perpetuating of dominant, and often harmful, societal narratives can happen across any mode or medium, multimodal textual forms have traditionally existed as sites of resistance to or disruption of these narratives. For example, graphic novels have overwhelmingly focused on the narratives of those least likely to have societal power, the approval of which has been borne out by both the popular and the critical embracing of Marjane Satrapi's (2003) *Persepolis*; John Lewis, Andrew Aydin, and Nate Powell's (2013) *March*; and, more recently, Mike Curato's (2020) *Flamer*. Digital multimodal texts that offer important information about political and social movements as well as space for individuals and organizations to post counternarratives can be found on a wide variety of accounts on Instagram, Twitter, or TikTok, and on websites like https://criticalmediaproject.org or https://www.justlitproject.com. In addition, zine-making has historically served as a multimodal opportunity for folks committed to various feminist, queer, and abolitionist movements and communities to share their (counter)stories.

A zine, derived from the word "fanzine," is a noncommercial, self-published work that is generally created by cutting and pasting images and text together by hand (although some people choose to create digital zines). While zines were first created by sci-fi enthusiasts in the early 20th century, they experienced waves of popularity in the 1970s and 1990s and continue to be a celebrated, if somewhat subversive, form—particularly for those whose voices are traditionally marginalized—used to disseminate information and serve as a creative, community-centered outlet.

In referencing the potential for multimodal forms of composition to encourage the creation of important counternarratives, Jen Scott Curwood and Damiana Gibbons (2010) write that "in accounting for multiple modes, researchers have found that nonprint texts are able to convey identity (or at least expressions of identity in the form of identity markers) in ways different from print texts" (p. 63) and that, particularly when encouraging children and youth to employ a critical stance, "the presence, absence, and co-occurrence of modes [can] function to create a multimodal counternarrative" (p. 66). They point to their examination of the digital poetry of a gay, Asian, and second-generation-immigrant high school student as well as the work of Kate Pahl (2011), Althea Scott Nixon (2009), and Nelson et al. (2008) to further validate their argument and call for literacy educators to use digital and multimodal invitations as "a way for youth to explore the master narratives around them, to push back against them, and to tell stories of their lives in an effort to (re)present their identities" (p. 74).

## Talking Back to the Naysayers

Despite everything I have laid out here, I am not so naive as to think that educators, administrators, and families will quietly accept a decentering of print-heavy forms of text in favor of developing a more inclusive space for students to make meaning across all modes. The power—and the supremacy—of the written word is real! Many will likely point to the standards they are expected to adhere to or the curricula they are required to use, which often make little to no mention of incorporating a wider variety of modalities in our instructional practice. However, I would carefully consider whether these pedagogical tools *actually* specify the use of exclusively alphabetic texts to teach students the skills, practices, and mindsets that qualify someone as being acceptably "literate," or if this is merely our own perception and/or assumptions at play. For example, to take a couple of Grade 3 standards from the *New Jersey Student Learning Standards for English Language Arts* (Department of Education, 2016), can we not teach children to "interpret words and phrases as they are used in a text, including determining technical, connotative, and figurative meanings, and analyze how specific word choices shape meaning or tone" (p. 1) using an online ad or an excerpt from a graphic novel? Can we not teach them to "write informative/explanatory texts to examine and convey complex ideas and information clearly and accurately through the effective selection, organization, and analysis of content" through the creation of a digital story or podcast? Of course we can. And if we want our students to effectively develop authentic, engaging, and inclusive practices for making meaning of our increasingly multimodal world, we must.

This work is decidedly *not* about eliminating print text from our schools or classrooms, but rather about understanding, and valuing, the varied and complex ways that individuals make meaning *while also* helping all students become adept at communicating utilizing a variety of modes. Additionally, it's about acknowledging and, when appropriate, disrupting the ways in which what has traditionally counted as "literacy"—for example, the reading and writing of print texts—has been used not just as a tool of liberation, particularly for those communities that have been historically marginalized, but as a tool of domination and oppression by those whose social, political, and economic power is dependent on it. We'll get into that more in Chapter 6.

### Internal Work
- Consider: What are the ways in which you, personally, make meaning across a variety of modes in your daily life? In what

ways are/were you taught and encouraged to become proficient in communicating effectively using more than just the alphabetic mode?

## External Work

- Where in your curriculum or instructional practice might you build in more opportunities for your students to read, analyze, and/or compose texts using different modalities? What kind of professional development or support do you need in order to do so? How might you and your colleagues engage in a fun, low-stakes mini-inquiry as a way of building capacity around this?
- Continue to jot what you are noticing about where literacy oppression "lives" in your district/school/classroom using the table from Chapter 1 as a guide.

# CHAPTER 6

# Literacy Can Be Used as a Tool for Liberation as Well as a Tool for Oppression

Our masters always tried to hide
Book learning from our eyes;
Knowledge didn't agree with slavery—
'Twould make us all too wise.
But some of us would try to steal
A little from the book.
And put the words together,
And learn by hook or crook.

—from Frances Ellen Watkins Harper (1992), "Learning to Read"

DOI: 10.4324/9781032658964-6

In her bestselling book *Bad Feminist*, award-winning writer Roxane Gay (2014) proudly and openly claims her identity as a "bad feminist" and shares how doing so has offered her a sense of liberation from the socially loaded label. In the introduction to her book, she writes:

> *I embrace the label of bad feminist because I am human. I am messy. I'm not trying to be an example. I am not trying to be perfect. I am not trying to say I have all the answers. I am not trying to say I am right. I am just trying—trying to support what I believe in, trying to do some good in this world, trying to make some noise with my writing while also being myself. (p. xi)*

While, like Gay, I too am a bad feminist (just ask my teenage daughters, who can likely point out with excruciating detail every flaw in my personal brand of feminism), I am also a bad advocate for literacy education. Or, at least, I sometimes feel that way. This is partly because, like Gay, I am messy. Messy in that on the one hand, I understand and value the ways in which literacy can be liberatory, particularly for those who have been historically marginalized or underserved. On the other hand, the more I adopt a critical stance as both an educator and a human being, the more I recognize the ways in which literacy can serve to perpetuate oppression and maintain the dominant social order. And because of this, my identity as a literacy educator is all wound up in a tight, messy, confusing ball of tension.

This last principle in my anti-oppressive literacy education framework—that literacy can be used as a tool for liberation *as well as* a tool for oppression—is, in my view, the most challenging to wrap our minds around, primarily because we don't *want* it to be this way. We don't *want* to have to acknowledge the ways that literacy—and literacy educators—can and do cause real, lasting harm. However, I also consider this last principle to be the most important of all five of them. In fact, I'm willing to assert my wholehearted belief that *we must, as literacy educators, seek to understand and embrace this principle above all others within the framework if we wish to have any hope of moving toward an anti-oppressive practice.*

If by this point you're still with me, my hunch is that you're at least willing to consider why I believe this to be true. For that, I am grateful.

Let's begin by looking back.

## Historicizing Literacy in the United States

The history of literacy is not easy to lay out in a clear and coherent manner, primarily because the murkiness around what constitutes "literacy"—and who has historically served as the arbiters around this—makes it a challenge (and somewhat of a nightmare for linear thinkers like me). However, when we focus on literacy as it developed in a particular place—for example, the stolen land that would eventually become the United States—it becomes slightly more manageable. I want to note here that I am choosing to focus on the history of *print literacy*, as this is the basket in which, as a practitioners, it seems we have collectively placed all of our "eggs" in terms of literacy's ability to transform both ourselves and our world over time.

### A NOTE ABOUT BRAILLE LITERACY

It's important to acknowledge the discourse among disability advocates and researchers around "the 'Braille literacy' gap" for legally blind individuals. In recent years, there has been a significant shift away from using braille in grades K–12 and a shift toward using speech-to-text and other assistive technologies. In a 2018 piece for the *Journal of Blindness Innovation and Research*, Arielle Michal Silverman and Edward C. Bell write that there are several reasons for this shift, including "a lack of braille competency among teachers, negative public attitudes toward braille for people with residual vision, increasing use of text-to-speech technology, and the increasing prevalence of multiple disabilities in blind children" (para. 1). They as well as others argue that technological advances that assist blind individuals in learning how to read and write should *supplement*, not supplant, the development of braille literacy, and that more inclusive literacy education for those who are visually

> impaired is essential for combating the "braille literacy crisis" (National Federation of the Blind, 2009).
>
> However, in a recent study of the citation practices of those writing about the rates of braille literacy among blind individuals, Rebecca M. Sheffield and her colleagues (2022) found that there is no "current source of data that succinctly measures braille literacy rates" in the United States and that therefore, whether braille literacy is *actually* declining or not is inconclusive (p. 1).

According to historians who've studied the number of signatures on colonial documents from the mid-1600s onward, a significant percentage of White men were considered to be "literate" during the late 17th/early 18th century—more so than those living in Europe at the time. This so-called "signature literacy" was considered by some to correlate with the ability to read print text fluently, although, according to professor of education, history, and public policy emeritus Carl F. Kaestle (1985), such a correlation "must be guarded" (p. 21). While a number of White women were also deemed to have some measure of signature literacy, this number plateaued in the mid-18th century and remained so for several decades. As for those who were not White—or more precisely, those who were not offered the "protection of Whiteness" (J. Borgioli-Binis, personal communication, June 3, 2022)—according to African American journalist and historian Carter G. Woodson (1919), by the late 1700s approximately 15%–20% of African Americans, for example, could read English-based print texts due to the efforts of free Black persons in establishing literary societies and schools for African American children, particularly in the Northeast.

For the most part, the sanctioned literacy of non-elite White European Americans during this time period was limited to what was necessary for being able to *access* and/or, for a select few, to *compose* religious, moral, and state-sanctioned print texts, such as property deeds, wills, and military enlistment records. As I wrote in Chapter 1, the print literacy education of Black folks, particularly after the surge in abolitionist sentiment following the Haitian Revolution (1791–1804) and, later, the Southampton Insurrection of 1831 (commonly known as Nat Turner's Rebellion), was either strictly controlled, or— in the case of those who were enslaved at the time—outright prohibited (Span, 2005, p. 27). This was largely due to White fear that, if enslaved Black persons were to develop the ability to read and write in English, more uprisings and/or rebellion would potentially occur, threatening the main source of America's economic growth and development. As African American studies scholar Heather A. Williams (2007) writes in her book *Self-Taught: African American Education in Slavery and Freedom,*

> *The presence of literate slaves threatened to give lie to the entire system [of chattel slavery]. Reading indicated to the world that this so-called property had a mind, and writing foretold the ability to construct an alternative narrative about bondage itself. Literacy among slaves would expose slavery, and masters knew it. (p. 7)*

An account of the 1831 insurrection, published in the *Richmond Compiler* two weeks after the incident, illustrates this belief:

> *A fanatic preacher, by the name of Nat. Turner [Gen. Nat. Turner!] who had been taught to read and write and permitted to go about preaching in the country, was at the bottom of this infernal brigandage. He was artful, impudent, and vindictive, without any cause or provocation that could be assigned. ("Insurrection of the Slaves," n.d., para. 4; bracketed comment in original)*

### The Rise of Antiliteracy Laws

Needless to say, the preposterous idea that enslaved Black folks would realize the inhumane conditions in which they were being forced to live and work (and therefore organize to abolish these conditions) *only* once they were able to read and write in English stuck, and most Confederate states passed or tightened strict antiliteracy laws in the years following the insurrection. (Despite this, as I also mentioned in Chapter 1, some enslaved Black children and adults in which these antiliteracy laws were passed were permitted to engage in "Bible literacy"—which purported to be valuable only in that it encouraged piety and adherence to Christian values—and many enslaved folks learned to read and write English through their own determination as well as through the subversive assistance of others.)

Interestingly, as I was drafting this chapter in the summer of 2022, National Public Radio (NPR) reported that the Michigan Department of Corrections banned Spanish and Swahili dictionaries from their penitentiaries. A quote from the department's spokesperson reads, "If certain prisoners all decided to learn a very obscure language, they would be able to then speak freely in front of staff and others about introducing contraband or assaulting staff" (Polo, 2022, para. 4). The NPR story goes on to say that the spokesperson indicated that "allowing prisoners to gain access to language books other than English could encourage them to organize without the knowledge of staff" (para. 5).

This state-sanctioned gatekeeping around print literacy practices in both the North and the South implied three things: one, that the development of print literacy outside of Bible literacy was seen as a commodity through which individuals could participate freely in civic life; two, that this commodity was one that revolved around the English language and that largely belonged only to those who were granted the protection of Whiteness; and three, that other literacy practices, such as those practiced by many Indigenous and African American folks, were considered insignificant or nonthreatening to White, Western ideologies (and consequently, the nation's burgeoning economy). For this and other reasons, literacy as it was defined by Whites became a double-edged sword for those whose racial, or racialized, identity was *not* White. Writing about this phenomenon in relation to enslaved Africans who developed the aforementioned Bible literacy, historical scholar Janet Cornelius writes:

*The religious context for learning [to read] was as important for slaves it was for owners; most slaves who learned to read on their own initiative did so in a religious context, demonstrating that Christian teachings and opportunities* could have liberating as well as conservative results. *(1983, pp. 173–174; my emphasis)*

While such literacy development enabled enslaved individuals to read texts that were *not* religious in nature (e.g., abolitionist texts), it also served, oppressively, as a tool for their indoctrination into the belief and value systems of those who had enslaved them (that is, into White, Euro-American notions of Christianity)—a belief system that included Bible-sanctioned justifications for slavery. (That is not to say that such indoctrination was always, or even sometimes, successful; in fact, it failed miserably, as evidenced by the number of enslaved folks who "reclaimed the Bible" [Weil, 2019] and its message of hope and spiritual liberation.)

Some of the undervalued literacy practices I reference here included those that made use of a variety of Indigenous languages (e.g., from the Algic and Iroquoian family of languages) as well as the home languages and pidgins of enslaved Africans. In addition, songs, stories, and other daily or ceremonial literacy practices of these communities—including the use of visual composition (e.g., pictographs)—were, and continue to be, dismissed or outright erased from dominant literacy ideologies.

Post–Civil War, literacy continued to be used both as a tool for liberation, as in the case of free Blacks demanding, developing, and subsidizing thousands of schools that made the literacy learning of students a priority (Butchart, 2020), and also as a tool for oppression—as when Whites who resented the 15th Amendment, which gave "citizens" (i.e., men) of the United States the right to vote regardless of their "race, color, or previous condition of servitude," began instituting literacy tests at the polls.

## BEYOND BLACK AND WHITE

While for the sake of space—and because the comprehensive subject of print literacy as a tool for both oppression and liberation is beyond the scope of this book—I focus this chapter primarily on the literacy experiences of African Americans, it is important to understand the ways that print literacy has also historically been used by Whites to oppress other racialized communities. For example, many readers are aware of the ways in which White educators at Indian boarding schools used English literacy as an assimilation tool in an attempt to ensure that Natives adopted the "sameness of sentiment and thought" of their colonizers (Gage, 2022). Despite such culturally violent intent, many Natives developed and appropriated English print literacy as a way to gain knowledge about the U.S. government and White culture as well as to resist colonization efforts. In fact, many Natives' development of English reading and writing practices became so widespread that it had an expansive effect on the U.S. Postal Service. On the companion website to his book *We Do Not Want the Gates Closed Between Us: Native Networks and the Spread of the Ghost Dance*, historian Justin Gage (2022) writes that in particular, "Western Native Americans turned the educational goals of the US government on its head, and used literacy to reestablish a sense of sovereignty, decolonize some aspects of their lives, and protect their tribes and families from colonial abuses."

## Literacy Gatekeeping Through Literacy Tests

In 1882, the state of South Carolina instituted the Eight Box Law, a de facto literacy test that required voters to place each of their eight ballots, one for each office (governor, senator, etc.), into the appropriate boxes—which were sometimes shuffled to purposely confuse those who could not read and to prevent print-literate do-gooders from helping their neighbors preemptively arrange their ballots in the proper order. In a 2022 blog post about the law that Faye Jensen composed for the South Carolina Historical Society, she writes:

> *Any vote miscast in the wrong box was voided. . . . Although election officials were supposedly required to read the [boxes'] labels upon request, that was randomly enforced. In some cases, election officials purposely misread the labels to voters. (para. 2)*

Literacy tests were also used to restrict immigration and, in doing so, protect the "purity" of the White (e.g., Anglo-Saxon) race, "upon which," eugenicist Madison Grant wrote in 1916, "the nation must chiefly depend for leadership, for courage, for loyalty, for unity and harmony of action" (p. xxxvii). These tests were considered by many in power to be so crucial in preventing the immigration of "undesirables" to the United States—largely identified as people of Eastern and Southern European as well as East Asian descent—that American sociologist Henry Pratt Fairchild (1917) wrote in his piece "The Literacy Test and Its Making" that "there can be no doubt that the agitation for the literacy test represents, in a very real way, the growing sentiment in favor of the actual restriction of immigration" (p. 452). In fact, he writes, the Immigration Commission, appointed by the House of Representatives in 1906, and after three years of research and nearly $1 million in spending, "unanimously recommended the restriction of immigration, and, with a single dissenting voice, *agreed that the best form of restriction was a literacy test*" (p. 456; my emphasis). (Note: Although the commission predicted that such a literacy test would exclude at least 40% of would-be immigrants, in reality, once such a test was voted into law in 1917, fewer than 1% were denied entry into the United States based on their level of print literacy [Boissoneault, 2017].)

## EUGENICS

Eugenics is the (scientifically debunked) practice, based in racism, antisemitism, ableism, and other oppressive prejudices, of attempting to control the reproductive practices of individuals in an effort to "improve" the genetic composition of the human race. The eugenics movement grew quickly in the United States starting in the late 1800s and is still visible in policies and practices today. For example, we can find traces of eugenics in forced-sterilization policies of incarcerated women as well as policies that have been put into place in the midst of the COVID-19 pandemic via the ending of transmission-mitigation efforts (despite the disproportionate vulnerability of people of color, the disabled, and children under 5).

For an excellent primer on the eugenics movement within the United States, I highly recommend Episode 8, "Skulls and Skin," of the "Seeing White" series from the *Scene on Radio* podcast (https://www .sceneonradio.org/episode-38-skulls-and-skins-seeing-white-part-8/).

While during the early part of the 20th century these proposed literacy tests generally consisted of reading an excerpt of the U.S. Constitution in the chosen language of the immigrant (and, in some cases, writing the sentences they could read), later on, before the passage of the Civil Rights Act of 1964, literacy tests once again became a tool used primarily for voter disenfranchisement—particularly the disenfranchisement of Black men—and included test items like

- a "reasonable interpretation" of the meaning of an excerpt of the state constitution, chosen by a (White) registrar (Mississippi, 1955);
- identifying where money is coined and how U.S. judges obtain their office (Louisiana, 1963);
- reciting the names of every federal district judge in the state (Georgia, circa 1958);
- identifying the number of individuals who, by law, must testify against a person charged with treason against the state (Alabama, circa 1960s).

In addition, would-be voters would be required to (1) read an excerpt of the state constitution chosen at the whim of the White registrar at the polls and (2) successfully fill out multiple forms that insisted on such nonessential information as the names of all of their employers up to the present day (Alabama), their mother's maiden name (Mississippi), and even the color of their own hair (South Carolina) (Hartford, n.d.).

As these assessment-focused examples of literacy-as-oppression illustrate, and as Amy J. Wan (2014) argues in her book *Producing Good Citizens: Literacy Training in Anxious Times*, the historical use of print literacy, and specifically print literacy tests, to confer or deny citizenship status—and with that, to confer or deny the benefits of citizenship (such as being able to engage in civic practices, like voting)—was essentially used "as a measure of personhood" (p. 3).

## Literacy Tests in Contemporary Times

Knowing how literacy tests in the past were used by folks to maintain White power, and even to distinguish who was White and who was not by virtue of the individual's perceived literacy proficiency (Prendergast, 2003), it is important to consider the ways in which this may still be the case today, albeit in a less explicit, more covert manner. For example, one could argue that those concerned with the United States' ongoing "literacy crisis" (see Figure 6.2)—a narrative that is perpetuated approximately every two years with the release of standardized literacy assessment data on a national scale and which, by the way, has been in play since the 1830s—are concerned only about the ability of Black, Brown, poor, multilingual, and/or disabled students to successfully access a level of functional literacy required to help them "succeed" in society. These folks often (implicitly) evoke the "literacy as a tool of liberation" narrative. One could *also* argue that these perpetual hand-wringers are, in effect, upholding the dominant power structure—i.e., using literacy as a tool of oppression— by *failing to question and/or disrupt the very standards for and measures of literacy proficiency themselves.* (In other words, while there absolutely *is* a literacy crisis in the United States, the dominant narrative fails to articulate the true reasons why this is the case.) Pointing specifically to the need for educators to disrupt the "science" of reading movement, for example—a movement that goes hand in hand with

Figure 6.2   The Dominant (U.S.) Literacy "Crisis" Narrative

the current literacy crisis narrative—scholar of urban teacher education H. Richard Milner IV writes:

> *The very foundation of what people even investigate as germane to knowing in and about reading had been shaped by White men, many of whom were historically eugenicists (Black, 2003). To be clear, similar to other fields of study, whiteness and maleness are at the very foundation of our understanding of the science of reading. (2020, p. S252)*

This is the case as well for those who have paved the way for us to consider what it means to be an "effective" or "good" writer, as award-winning educator Felicia Rose Chavez (2021) reminds us in her book *The Anti-Racist Writing Workshop: How to Decolonize the Creative Classroom*. In the book's introduction, echoing the sentiment of Milner when discussing the science of reading, Chavez asserts that, for teachers of writing, "it is time to admit that writing is a political, historical, and ideological act steeped in identity politics" (p. 10).

## Sanctioned Uses of Literacy

A significant difference, however, between (1) the development of a practice of reading and writing and (2) who has historically been granted access to either print literacy practice, is how its uses have been sanctioned. Remember that for enslaved Black persons, reading for the purposes of religious/moral enlightenment was deemed acceptable by many White folks. This was also the case for Native children who were forced to attend Indian boarding schools; in the December 20, 1903, edition of the *St. Paul Globe*, for example, it was written that "the school book and the Bible are doing more towards civilizing the [r-slur] than the soldiers in Uncle Sam's army have been able to do" ("Indians Who Refuse," para. 14). Alternatively, writing, according to composition scholar Deborah Brandt (2014), "has always been less *for* good than it is *a* good" (p. 5)—in other words, has consistently been perceived as a resource or commodity used to share knowledge, communicate ideas across time and space, and govern and control groups of people (through treaties, contracts, laws, literature, and so forth). In this way, one could argue, the gatekeeping of writing over time—through both *denial of access* and *dominant norms around what writing should look/sound like* (e.g., which writing practices have historically been sanctioned in schools [see Chapter 5])—has also historically served as a form of opportunity hoarding by White elites, even as other, non-White communities have accepted, embraced, and—in many cases—reappropriated these sanctioned practices. In the book *We Lived in a Little Cabin in the Yard* (Hurmence, 1994), a set of firsthand accounts by formerly enslaved people who were interviewed by members of the 1930s-era Federal Writers' Project, Joseph Holmes, 81 at the time of his interview, related the following:

*Old Miss taught the [n————s] how to read and write, and some of them got to be too efficient with the writing—they learn how to write too many passes so the pattyrollers [members of the slave patrols] wouldn't get them. That was the onliest time I ever knowed old Miss to have the slaves punished. (pp. 16–17)*

While many of us (perhaps) wish to believe that the gatekeeping around both reading and writing is something relegated to our "less-enlightened" past, our current educational system continues to demonstrate the ways in which literacy is used to oppress those whose identities are not the most privileged or that have the least amount of social, cultural, and political power. For example, scholars like Anne Haas Dyson have pointed out numerous times how literacy instruction that is "focused on the basics . . . [is] most visible in schools serving low-income children." The problem with this, as she and others (e.g., Haberman, 1991) have argued, is that such a focus "too often [yields] a bare-bones education . . . that writes out of consideration the particularities of children's lives" (Dyson, 2013, p. 5). Karolyn Tyson, professor of sociology and the author of the 2011 book *Integration Interrupted: Tracking, Black Students, and Acting White After Brown*, found in her study of 250 students in more than 30 elementary and secondary schools across the Southeast that "racialized tracking systems" continue to play a significant role in the education of Black students:

> *Tracking does more than keep black and white students separated during the school day. It also produces and maintains a set of conditions in which academic success is linked with whites: students equate achievement with whiteness because school structures do. (p. 6)*

Although we would like to believe otherwise, over a decade after Tyson's book was published, American schools have only become more segregated. A 2020 study by the National Center for Analysis of Longitudinal Data in Education Research (CALDER) found that, in North Carolina at least, classroom-level segregation *within schools*— particularly at the middle and high school level—was sharply divided along color lines, with Black and Brown children much more likely to be enrolled in "rudimentary" classes than White children (Clotfelter et al., 2021, p. 1) and with emergent bilinguals being the most affected by such segregation. This study echoes the work of those who have tracked racial and ethnic disparities in students receiving opportunities to enroll in "gifted" or advanced placement classes, with White students more likely to be enrolled in both kinds of programs (Grissom & Reading, 2016; Groeger et al., 2018). Because literacy often serves as a "proxy" for education (and vice versa), it stands to reason that if a large number of students of color continue to be segregated from White students in many U.S. classrooms *in general,* we can quite comfortably assume that this segregation—and alongside it, a less rich, more "back to basics" type of curriculum—*also* exists when it comes to the kinds of literacy instruction students receive in school spaces.

## OPPORTUNITY HOARDING

First coined by sociologist Charles Tilly in 1998, "opportunity hoarding" is a phenomenon whereby members of a privileged or dominant "in-group" gatekeep or limit a "value-producing resource" (Voss, 2010, p. 369) for others, thus perpetuating inequity. "Over the long run of human history," Tilly writes, "a wide variety of value-producing resources have sometimes served as bases of categorical inequality-generation," such as those with limited supply (e.g., water, food, and housing) (p. 35). Although the practices of reading and writing are not, per se, limited resources, rising literacy demands over time and the historical devaluing of the kinds of home or community literacy practices that many traditionally marginalized people engage in in school spaces can be considered a form of opportunity hoarding, especially when high stakes (such as test scores, academic credits, or college admissions) are attached to the ability to successfully assimilate to the sanctioned literacy practices of the dominant in-group.

To understand more about how the opportunity hoarding of elites is used to maintain inequity and stymie the social mobility of those living in poverty, check out the interactive simulation "Are You a Dream Hoarder?" on the Brookings Institution website (https://www.brookings .edu/interactives/are-you-a-dream-hoarder/).

## Text Access

Not only have those with dominant social identities—and consequently, the most social power—historically tried to maintain control over the kinds of literacy *practices* that people engage in; the same can be said for the kinds of *texts that people have access to*. As I am writing this chapter, in the spring of 2022, we are witnessing an unprecedented rise in the number of book challenges and bans that have taken place in classrooms and in libraries across the country (Mazariegos & Sullivan, 2022), which, it can be argued, is in response to perceived gains in the embracing of literature that focuses on historically marginalized stories and experiences thanks to the work of movements like #DisruptTexts, #OwnVoices, and #WeNeedDiverseBooks. Although both the formal and the informal challenging of books and other print texts is not new, the vast majority of the challenges that are currently being made by mostly White, conservative Americans are targeting texts that feature a protagonist/author that identifies as a member of a particular LGBTQIA+ community and/or is Black. In some cases, individuals or groups are even moving beyond civil actions (e.g., writing letters/emails or speaking at school board meetings) and filing criminal complaints as a way to remove certain books from schools and libraries, including a school board member in Florida who claims that George M. Johnson's (2020) award-winning memoir *All Boys Aren't Blue* violates the state's obscenity laws for "[including] descriptions of masturbation, oral and anal sex and sexual assault" (Alexander, 2021, para. 4). In the book's third act, the author does indeed recount how they were sexually assaulted by an older cousin at the age of 13 and, later, by a classmate at their high school—and how this traumatic event led to their awareness (and years-long suppression of) their attraction to boys. However, many—including the author themselves—would argue that, far from harming any minor who reads it, the book actually offers a way for victims of sexual assault, particularly those who are Black and queer, to understand that they are not alone. In short, the wave of people lodging state-level criminal complaints (in Florida, Oklahoma, Virginia, Utah, and Texas, to name just a few) as part of a concerted attempt to remove books like *All Boys Aren't Blue* from school and community libraries amounts to little more than political theater and encourages a disingenuous interpretation of these states' obscenity and/or pornography laws.

## BOOK BANS: A LONG TRADITION

It can reasonably be argued that as long as there have been books, there have been book bans. Here are just a few examples of how this censorship practice has enjoyed a long history:

- In 213 BCE, China's first emperor, Qin Shi Huang, ordered that a number of books on history and philosophy be burned (at the suggestion of his political ally, Li Ssu) in order to distract from "divergent schools of political and social thought" (Chan, 1972).
- In the early 15th century, King James I of England banned Sir Walter Raleigh's *The History of the World* for "being too saucy."
- In the United States, books and other print texts were burned or banned throughout the 17th, 18th, and 19th centuries for reasons that include: (1) being critical of Puritanism, (2) providing women with reproductive advice, (3) being pro-abolitionist (as in the case of Harriet Beecher Stowe's *Uncle Tom's Cabin*), and so forth.
- In the 1930s, student groups across Germany who were also Nazi sympathizers burned books that were deemed to be anti-German and/or whose authors were Jewish. In addition, one of the Nazis' first shows of force against Germany's LGBTQ+ community was a raid on the libraries of the German Institute of Sexology, destroying vital research around gender affirmation studies and other important records of members of the LGBTQ+ community.
- As mentioned in Chapter 5, during the 1950s, many comic books were burned or banned in the United States for "corrupting" America's youth (despite the fact that the majority of comic enthusiasts at the time were adult men).
- During the Reagan administration there was an enormous surge in book bans and challenges, partially as a response to the increase in more permissive and/or explicit art during the 1960s and 1970s. In 1982, the American Library Association celebrated its first Banned Books Week.

What is objectively oppressive about the systematic removal of books from a school or community library? According to the Committee on Professional Ethics (COPE) of the American Library Association (ALA), libraries "have a special obligation to ensure the free flow of information and ideas to present and future generations" (ALA, 2009) and thus uphold Americans' First Amendment right to free speech. As such, the successful removal of a text from a library violates this right. However, many folks would argue that the removal of, say, an antisemitic or White supremacist text is not inherently oppressive— that challenges of books like *The Poisonous Mushroom* (1938) or *The Turner Diaries* (1978) are *actually positive* in that they aim to censor ideas that are not protected by the First Amendment, such as those that may be deemed "legally obscene" or "fighting words . . . which by their very utterance inflict injury or tend to incite an immediate breach of the peace" (American Civil Liberties Union, n.d., para. 18). While this may certainly *feel* true, when we think about how some forms of hate speech can be construed as including so-called fighting words, this becomes even more complicated when we consider who is making, and who has historically made, the most prominent decisions around what kinds of texts fall under these specific unprotected categories.

In case you are unfamiliar with some of the titles I mention in this chapter, *The Poisonous Mushroom* (1938) is an antisemitic children's book that attempts to warn its readers about Jewish people and the "danger" they pose. *The Turner Diaries* (1978) is a dystopian novel that depicts a White supremacist attempt to overthrow the government. It is said to have been the inspiration behind both the 1996 Oklahoma City bombing as well as the January 6, 2021, attack on the U.S. Capitol building.

## Patterns of Censorship

Therefore, what I would invite us to focus on, and do some exploratory work around (alongside our students!), are the patterns that exist in the censorship of books and other print texts over time. If we were to identify such patterns—that would be made visible from considering *who* has challenged *which* texts (in *what* spaces) and *why*—we would quickly recognize, I think, that this particular practice is one that, overwhelmingly, protects the ideas and beliefs of those that hold dominant identities—particularly that of White, conservative Christians— and explicitly targets beliefs, ideas, and stories that disrupt them, particularly within schools. For example, when looking at the most oft-challenged books of the 20th century and the reasons cited for these challenges, as documented by the American Library Association (2013), we see things like:

- *The Catcher in the Rye* (1951) being challenged by a group of parents at a school board meeting for being "profane," "anti-white," and for promoting "immorality";
- *The Grapes of Wrath* (1939) challenged by a parent at a North Carolina high school for "taking the Lord's name in vain" and for being "full of filth";
- *Brave New World* (1932) challenged by a high school parent for "show[ing] contempt for religion, marriage, and family";
- *Animal Farm* (1945) challenged by members of the John Birch Society, a right-wing political advocacy group, because its author is a "communist"; and
- *Native Son* (1940) challenged by a group of California parents for being "unnecessarily violent and sexually explicit."

And while many books have also been challenged over the past century for reasons like "including ethnic, racist, or sexist slurs" (e.g., *To Kill a Mockingbird, Of Mice and Men*) or "depicting bestiality" (e.g., *Beloved, One Flew Over the Cuckoo's Nest*), what is both interesting and disheartening to note is how, over the past decade or so, these challenges have more and more frequently focused on the growing number of texts that feature people or characters who identify as gay, queer, or transgender, with the most challenged book of 2021 being Maia Kobabe's (2019) award-winning graphic memoir *Gender Queer*, a book that explores the author's confusion around eir* gender and sexual identity. Although many of those who object to these books (and more specifically, their place in school and public libraries) claim to do so due to the frank depiction and/or discussion of sexuality in general, and not to what has been characterized as "LGBTQ content" (Alter, 2022), the fervor around depictions of heterosexuality in books like those that Stephenie Meyer (the *Twilight* series), John Green (*The Fault in Our Stars, Looking for Alaska*), or Sarah J. Maas (the *Court of Thorn and Roses* series) is unmatched by the current and historical fervor around queer sex and sexuality.

*For those who are unaware, the pronouns Kobabe has used since 2016, when e began coming out to friends and family as nonbinary, are e, eir, and em.

## Literacy as Liberation: A Way Forward

Despite what we now know about just some of the ways that literacy has historically been—and continues to be—used as a tool of oppression, mainly by White elites, we can take heart in *also knowing* how literacy can be used as a tool for liberation.

For that, we would do well to take a page from the very communities who have spent centuries collectively resisting the use of literacy as a tool of oppression—often at great risk to their own lives—and who in most cases did not need any paternalistic outside intervention to illuminate or disrupt the oppression they were experiencing (and continue to experience). These include the Western Native American communities I referenced earlier in this chapter, who made use of their own Native languages and, at the same time, independently learned and used their colonizers' print and English-language-based literacy practices to build intertribal, continent-spanning print-communication networks through the U.S. Postal Service (Gage, 2022). They also include the efforts of Indigenous communities outside of the United States who demanded the preservation of Indigenous knowledges and literacies and/or "hybrid" literacies in the wake of "Freirean-inspired" literacy campaigns in places like Bolivia and Guinea-Bissau (Kee & Carr-Chellman, 2019). Rather than embrace these well-intentioned, but ultimately harmful, campaigns—which threatened to "[reproduce] Western hegemonic assumptions [about literacy] in the name of liberation" and marginalize Indigenous literacy practices (p. 98)—these communities instead enacted literacy pedagogies that centered the interests and practices of youth and honored their existing linguistic traditions while also reflecting on the ways in which these practices and traditions *were* or *were not* embodied in dominant educational systems.

## FREIREAN-INSPIRED WHAT, NOW?

"Freirean-inspired" is a reference to the work of Brazilian educator and activist Paulo Freire, who famously advocated for the enacting of "critical pedagogies" as a way to disrupt and dismantle the dehumanization of the oppressed. Critical pedagogy rejects what Freire calls "the "banking model of education," which treats students as empty vessels waiting to be filled with "knowledge," and instead embraces a pedagogy that encourages curiosity, consciousness-raising, and an egalitarian relationship among *all* members of the learning community.

However illuminating Freire's work was and continues to be, it is important to note that he has been criticized for his and his supporters' paternalistic attempts to impose their assumptive and colonialist views of literacy, in particular, on many rural communities during the 1970s and 1980s.

In short, these Indigenous communities, alongside a great number of others (e.g., the Mi'kmaq, Hopi/Tewa, and Diné Nations), engaged in what scholars have called critical Indigenous pedagogy (CIP), which "utilizes pedagogical methods that are critical, self-reflexive, dialogical, decolonizing and transformative while valuing and relying on Indigenous knowledge systems to promote, protect and preserve Indigenous languages, cultures, land and people" (Garcia & Shirley, 2012). CIP builds upon and extends the concept of critical pedagogy through an emphasis on "giving back" to Indigenous communities in a way that seeks to protect tribal sovereignty.

## Literacy as a "Collective Pursuit"

In examining the historical and current literacy practices of a number of African American communities, we can also find an emphasis on acknowledging, honoring, and centering Afrocentric knowledges and experiences as well as on literacy as a collective pursuit (Muhammad, 2020). For example, in her book *In Pursuit of Knowledge: Black Women and Educational Activism in Antebellum America*, Dr. Kabria Baumgartner (2019) tells the stories of countless African American women throughout the 19th century who fiercely advocated for the right of *all* children and youth to receive a public school education in the United States. Far from simply being "a path to literacy," she writes, education was "a force multiplier allowing African American men, women and children to live their purpose" (p. 7). And as Dr. Gholdy Muhammad writes in reference to the development of Black literary societies at this same time,

> *although individual literacy was valued [among African Americans] "if one person . . . acquired knowledge, it was then his or her responsibility to pass it on to others [as a way to] elevate . . . the larger community. (2020, p. 26)*

This is illustrated in the ways that enslaved Africans shared with one another what few English literacy skills they were able to develop under the oppression of chattel slavery; in the ways that free Black persons tirelessly advocated for the democratization of public schools for all during and post-Reconstruction; in the evolution of the Harlem Renaissance of the 1920s and the Black Arts Movement of the 1960s; and in the creation of Black publishing houses and independent Black institutions (IBIs) throughout U.S. history. In these and countless other ways, so many African American literate traditions, many of which reappropriated White-sanctioned literacy practices as a tool for African Americans' own liberation, "represent the intersections of literacy, education, and activism" (Fisher, 2004, p. 299).

This tradition of melding literacy pedagogy and practice with the pursuit of collective liberation lives on through current scholarship. For example, it lives on in Dr. Kim Parker's development of what she calls Culturally Relevant Intentional Literacy Communities (CRILCs) in K–12 classrooms, which are characterized by student choice, critical engagement, and sociopolitical activism as well as by a sense of collectivism where everyone within the CRILC "is guided by a spirit of belonging to one another, of being responsible for one another [and] of being invested in the long-term flourishing of one another" (2022, p. 60). It also lives on in Lorena Germán's (2021) conceptualization of "Textured Teaching," which includes as one of its four central traits a focus on both student-driven and community-centered literacy pedagogy. And it lives on in a wide variety of learning spaces outside of school buildings—on social media, in basement coffeehouses, on street corners, and within the hearts and minds of those committed to the cause of literacy for all.

As Germán writes in her bestselling book *Textured Teaching* (2021), "Community-driven teaching requires that [we] consider [our] own positionality, what community [we] are teaching in, and how this plays a role in the curriculum" (p. 25). Like those whose work around school-community partnerships I cited in my introduction, Germán encourages teachers to design units around local community issues and to make it a habit to invite members of the community, including families, into our classrooms in order to engage students in a variety of diverse knowledges, practices, and perspectives.

As history has shown us, despite the best intentions of those who have tried (and despite what I myself believed at one time), it is simply not enough to provide individuals with the literacy "skills" necessary to "participate effectively" in our White, Euro-American, cis-hetero-dominated society. It is not enough—or even the least bit appropriate—to simply teach our students the "languages and literacies of power" at the cost of, or to the detriment of, their own languages and literacies (and, if they're White, to the detriment of a richer, more inclusive understanding of literacy). And while there is no tried-and-true step-by-step process, procedure, or set of Blackline Masters for creating the kinds of liberatory literacy spaces in schools and classrooms that our students deserve, we can—at the very least—move toward the enactment of these spaces by collectively, and *actively*, committing to

- recognizing, acknowledging, and teaching our students the ways in which literacy has been used, and continues to be used, as a tool of oppression;
- honoring and centering the languages and literacy practices of historically marginalized communities (regardless of the student populations with which we work);
- keeping our students—and their particular identities, experiences, and interests—at the core of our literacy pedagogy;
- contextualizing literacy within our past and current sociocultural realities; and
- using literacy as a tool not only for disrupting and dismantling oppressive systems but also for collectively reimagining new systems.

Despite all the noise around literacy education that is designed to distract us from what really matters, I truly believe that, as literacy educators with a collective amount of professional expertise, political might, and social capital, *we can do this*. And more importantly—we must.

### Internal Work
- Acknowledging, first, that so many of you already have a vast knowledge base around literacy, what did you learn from this chapter that you perhaps *didn't* already know? Think about how this new (or broader) knowledge might shape or shift your practice as an educator.
- Awareness and acknowledgment are important to changing one's

mindset—and ultimately, one's practices. As a literacy educator, I have, in the past, *simultaneously* used literacy as a tool for liberation (e.g., when advocating for specialized literacy instruction for my students with dyslexia) and as a tool for oppression (e.g., when upholding unnecessarily rigid beliefs around "Standard" English). When have you used literacy as a tool for liberation and/ or oppression?

## External Work

- Having identified and acknowledged where literacy oppression "lives" in your district/school/classroom, create a shared set of goals that you and your colleagues will commit to working toward throughout your time together as educators. How will you begin? Where might you and your colleagues need to engage in more inquiry or scholarship? And most importantly, how will you hold yourself accountable to yourselves, your students, and the communities that you serve? Feel free, if you haven't done so already, to use the AOLitEd Framework Worksheet I have provided (see appendix) as a guide.

# CONCLUSION

*Engaged pedagogy does not seek simply to empower students. Any classroom that employs a holistic model of learning will also be a place where teachers grow, and are empowered by the process.*
—bell hooks (1994), *Teaching to Transgress: Education as the Practice of Freedom*

As a child, I dreamed of one day publishing a book of my own. The book I always thought I would write and publish would be a wry yet heartwarming take on my own life as well as on life in general—kind of like Amy Krouse Rosenthal's *Encyclopedia of an Ordinary Life* if she hadn't (brilliantly) gotten to it first. While this particular book has yet to materialize for me, I take heart in knowing that by the end of 2023—if I don't royally screw things up in the next 6–12 months—I will have written and published *three* professional books for educators.

Did I work hard to accomplish this? Of course. Writing a book—even one that *never has* or *never will* see the light of day—is no small feat! Was I also helped along, every step of the way, by the professional, social, linguistic, and even financial capital I've accrued from the very moment I was conceived, as a result of being a White, cis, able-bodied individual?

You bet your sweet bippy I was.

Sometimes called "cumulative advantage" (Crystal & Shea, 1990) and sometimes the "Matthew Effect," the concept is the same: Those who are advantaged at the outset—through the (often unearned) pro-curement of different forms of capital or access—continue to benefit from these advantages, compounding inequity over time. This plays out in a wide variety of societal systems and institutions—in publishing, in health care, in the legal system, and (surprise!) in education. As I have attempted to demonstrate throughout these chapters, children whose literacy and language practices match those that have historically been, and continue to be, centered in school spaces are the ones that most often benefit from being immersed in these spaces 5 days a week, 7 hours a day, 170 days a year, for 16-plus years. The extent to which this happens is enormous, and this doesn't even take into account other factors—factors like access to healthy and culturally familiar food, having reliable transportation to and from school, and so on.

The good news is, it doesn't have to be this way. As both bestselling author Heather McGhee and Atlanta Public Schools chief equity and social justice officer Dr. Tauheedah Baker-Jones have said (McGhee, 2021; Baker-Jones & Bouffard, 2021), the broader work of dismantling oppression is not a "zero-sum" game. Just because we choose, for example, to *decenter* the ideologies and assumptions that prevent educators from seeing and honoring the full humanity of their students doesn't mean that some will lose out; quite the contrary. *We all win*— our students and ourselves—when we actively work toward enacting anti-oppressive policies, practices, and pedagogies both in and outside of schools. This is the case in all aspects of education, but it is *especially* the case in literacy education, which affects nearly every other kind of learning.

Of course, I am not so naive as to think that reading this book— and even incorporating every suggestion I make within it—is going to make literacy education anti-oppressive. As I said in the introduction, sustained change does not happen in a vacuum, and it doesn't happen overnight. This work, and the larger work of disrupting oppression, takes time, effort, discipline, and sacrifice—*particularly* for those who, like me, hold a variety of socially powerful identities. It takes community and a willingness to be held accountable to one's communities. In addition, it takes a commitment to engage in joyful dreaming— dreaming of more inclusive, equitable, and just systems.

And sometimes, all it takes to *begin* this work is a little nudge. Consider this your nudge.

# REFERENCES

Ackerman, D. J., Barnett, W. S., & Robin, K. B. (2005). *Making the most of kindergarten: Present trends and future issues in the provision of full-day programs*. National Institute for Early Education Research.

Addy, N. D. A. (2018). *A multiple case study of early language and literacy practices in Black middle class families in the southeastern United States: Implications of race and class* [Doctoral dissertation, University of North Carolina at Chapel Hill]. Carolina Digital Repository. https://cdr.lib.unc.edu

Afflerbach, P. (2018). *Understanding and using reading assessment K–12* (3rd ed.). Association for Supervision and Curriculum Development.

Alexander, C. (2021, November 17). Flagler Schools book ban controversy: Sheriff investigating possible criminal charges. *The Daytona Beach News-Journal*. https://www.news-journalonline.com/story/news/education/2021/11/17/flagler-sheriff-investigating-possible-criminal-charges-related-book/8645651002/

Alexander, F. (2013). A perpetual literacy crisis? Bourgeois fears, working-class realities, and pedagogical responses. *Open Words: Access and English Studies, 7*(1), 41–51.

Alim, H. S., & Paris, D. (2015). Whose language gap? Critical and culturally sustaining pedagogies as necessary challenges to racializing hegemony. *Journal of Linguistic Anthropology, 25*(1), 79–81.

Allen, K. C. (2014). *Breaking the "at risk" code: Deconstructing the myth and the label* [Doctoral dissertation, Loyola Marymount University]. LMU/LLS Theses and Dissertations, 196. https://digitalcommons.lmu.edu/etd/196

Alter, A. (2022, May 1). How a debut graphic memoir became the most banned book in the country. *The New York Times*. https://

www.nytimes.com/2022/05/01/books/maia-kobabe-gender-queer
-book-ban.html

American Civil Liberties Union. (n.d.). *Freedom of expression.* https://
www.aclu.org/other/freedom-expression

American Library Association. (2009, October 28). *Committee on professional ethics (COPE).* http://www.ala.org/aboutala/committees/
ala/ala-profethic

American Library Association. (2013, March 26). *Banned & challenged classics.* http://www.ala.org/advocacy/bbooks/frequently
challengedbooks/classics

Anderson, C. (2016). *White rage: The unspoken truth of our racial divide.*
Bloomsbury.

Anderson, K. T., & Kachorsky, D. (2019). Assessing students' multimodal compositions: An analysis of the literature. *English Teaching Practice & Critique, 18*(3). https://doi.org/10.1108/ETPC-11
-2018-0092

Arnold, R., Burke, B., James, C., Martin, D., & Thomas, B. (1991).
*Educating for a change.* Between the Lines.

Bailey, M., & Trudy. (2018). On misogynoir: Citation, erasure, and
plagiarism. *Feminist Media Studies, 18*(4), 762–768.

Baker-Bell, A. (2020). *Linguistic justice: Black language, literacy, identity, and pedagogy.* National Council of Teachers of English.

Baker-Jones, T., & Bouffard, S. (2021, December). Equity work is not
a zero-sum game. *The Learning Professional.* https://learningforward
.org/journal/leading-for-equity/equity-work-is-not-a-zero
-sum-game/

Barnett, T. (2000)" Reading "whiteness" in English studies. *College
English, 63*(1), 9–37.

Baumgartner, K. (2019). *In pursuit of knowledge: Black women and educational activism in antebellum America.* New York University Press.

Bellanger, B. (1997). Methods of memory: On Native American storytelling. *College English, 59*(7), 789–800.

Belt-Beyan, P. M. (2004). *The emergence of African American literary
traditions: Family and community efforts in the nineteenth century.*
Westport, CT: Praeger.

Betts, E. A., Dolch, E. W., Gates, A. I., Gray, W. S., Horn, E., Brant,

L. L., Roberts, H., Smith, D. V., Smith, N. B., & Witty, P. (1942). What shall we do about reading today? A symposium. *The Elementary English Review, 19*(7), 225–256.

Biewen, J. (Host, Executive Producer.) (2015–present). *Scene on radio* [Audio podcast]. Center for Documentary Studies at Duke University.

Bishop, R. S. (1990). Mirrors, windows, and sliding glass doors. *Perspectives, 6*(3), ix–xi.

Boissoneault, L. (2017, February 6). Literacy tests and Asian exclusion were the hallmarks of the 1917 Immigration Act. *Smithsonian Magazine* (online). https://www.smithsonianmag.com/history/how-america-grappled-immigration-100-years-ago-180962058/

Brandt, D. (2004). Drafting U.S. literacy. *College English, 66*(5), 485–502.

Brandt, D. (2014). *The rise of writing: Redefining mass literacy.* Cambridge University Press.

Brem, S., Bach, S., & Kucian, K. (2010, April 15). Brain sensitivity to print emerges when children learn letter–speech sound correspondences. *Proceedings of the National Academy of Sciences, 107*(17), 7939–7944.

Bremner, R. H. (Ed.). (1970). *Children and youth in America: A documentary history: Vol. 1. 1600–1865.* Harvard University Press.

Brown, M. W. (1942). *The runaway bunny.* HarperCollins.

Bui, T. (2012). *Immigrant students use cartoons to share their journeys.* What Kids Can Do. http://www.whatkidscando.org/featurestories/2012/03_oakland_international/index.html

Butchart, R. (2020). Freedmen's education during Reconstruction. *New Georgia Encyclopedia*, last modified September 16, 2020. https://www.georgiaencyclopedia.org/articles/history-archaeology/freedmens-education-during-reconstruction/

Bryan, J., Williams, J. M., & Griffin, D. (2020). Fostering educational resilience and opportunities in urban schools through equity-focused school–family–community partnerships. *Professional School Counseling, 23*(1, part 2), 1–14.

Cappello, M., Wiseman, A. M., & Turner, J. D. (2019). Framing equitable classroom practices: Potentials of critical multimodal literacy research. *Literacy Research: Theory, Method, and Practice*, *68*(1), 205–225.

Carter, P., & Welner, K. (2013, May 13). It's the opportunity gap, stupid. *New York Daily News.* https://www.nydailynews.com/opinion/opportunity-gap-stupid-article-1.1340946

Carter, S. (2006). Redefining literacy as a social practice. *Journal of Basic Writing, 25*(2), 94–125.

Chan, L. M. (1972). The burning of the books in China, 213 B.C. *The Journal of Library History, 7*(2), 101–108.

Chavez, F. R. (2021). *The anti-racist writing workshop: How to decolonize the creative classroom.* Haymarket Books.

Children's Reading Foundation. (n.d.). *If you could close the school readiness gap, would you?* Ready for Kindergarten. https://try.readingfoundation.org/

Children's Reading Foundation. (2015). *Conquering the readiness gap.* http://www.readingfoundation.org/mailchimp/Conquering%20the%20Readiness%20Gap%20READY!%20for%20Kindergarten.pdf

Chinook Fund. (n.d.). *General terms & forms of oppression.* Retrieved February 15, 2022, from https://chinookfund.org/wp-content/uploads/2015/10/Supplemental-Information-for-Funding-Guidelines.pdf

Clark, E. E. (2017). Are comics effective materials for teaching ELLs? A literature review on graphic media for L2 instruction. *International E-Journal of Advances in Education, 3*(8), 298–309.

Clifford, G. J. (1984).Buchessen und lesen: Historical perspectives on literacy and schooling. *Review of Educational Research, 45*(4), 472–500.

Clotfelter, C., Ladd, H., Clifton, C. R., & Turaeva, M. R. (2021). *School segregation at the classroom level in a southern "new destination" state.* (CALDER Working Paper No. 230-0220-3). National Center for Analysis of Longitudinal Data in Education Research.

Coleman, J., Campbell, E., Hobson, C., McPartland, J., Mood, A., Weinfeld, F. D., & York, R. L. (1966). *Equality of educational opportunity.* Department of Health, Education and Welfare.

Collins, J. (1989). Hegemonic practice: Literacy and standard language in public education. *Journal of Education, 171*(2), 9–34.

Connors, S. P. (2010). "The best of both worlds": Rethinking the literary merit of graphic novels. *The ALAN Review, 65*–70.

Conroy, R. (2021, October 12). *The role of implicit bias: Dyslexia diagnosis and race.* The Windward Institute. https://www.thewindwardschool .org/the-windward-institute/the-beacon/article/-board/beacon -archives/post/the-role-of-implicit-bias-dyslexia-diagnosis-and-race

Cook-Gumperz, J. (1986). Literacy and schooling: An unchanging equation? In J. Cook-Gumperz (Ed.), *The Social Construction of Literacy.* Cambridge University Press.

Cook-Gumperz, J. & Keller-Cohen, K. (1993). Alternative literacies in school and beyond: Multiple literacies of speaking and writing. *Anthropology & Education Quarterly, 24*(4), 283–287.

Cope, B., & Kalantzis, M. (2015). *The things you do to know: An introduction to the pedagogy of multiliteracies.* Macmillan.

Core Knowledge Foundation. (2010). *Core knowledge sequence: Content and skill guidelines for Grades K–8.* https://www.coreknowledge .org/wp-content/uploads/2016/09/CKFSequence_Rev.pdf

Cornelius, J. (1983). We slipped and learned to read: Slave accounts of the literacy process, 1830–1865. *Phylon, 44*(3), 171–186.

Coppola, S. (2019). *Writing, redefined: Broadening our ideas of what it means to compose.* Stenhouse.

Crenshaw, K. (1989). Demarginalizing the intersection of race and sex: A black feminist critique of antidiscrimination doctrine, feminist theory and antiracist politics. *University of Chicago Legal Forum, 1*(Article 8), 139–167.

Cruz, C. (2015). *The unstoppable writing teacher: Real strategies for the real classroom.* Heinemann.

Cuban, L. (1989). The "at-risk" label and the problem of urban school reform. *Phi Delta Kappan, 70.*

Curato, M. (2020). *Flamer.* Henry Holt.

Curwood, J. S., & Gibbons, D. (2010). "Just like I have felt": Multimodal counternarratives in youth-produced digital media. *International Journal of Learning and Media, 2*(1), 59–77.

Darling-Hammond, L., & Adams, R. (2014). *Beyond the bubble test: How performance assessments support 21st century learning.* Jossey-Bass.

Dehaene, S. (2011). The massive impact of literacy on the brain and its consequences for education. *Human Neuroplasticity and Education.* https://www.unicog.org/publications/Dehaene%20Review%20 Cognitive%20neuroscience%20of%20Reading%20and%20 Education%202011.pdf

Delpit, L. (1988). The silenced dialogue: Power and pedagogy in educating other people's children. *Harvard Educational Review, 53*(3), 280–298.

Delpit, L. (2002). *The skin that we speak: Thoughts on language and culture in the classroom.* The New Press.

Deniz, F., Nunez-Elizalde, A. O., Huth, A. G., & Gallant, J. L. (2019, September 25). The representation of semantic information across human cerebral cortex during listening versus reading is invariant to stimulus modality. *The Journal of Neuroscience, 39*(39), 7722–7736.

Department of Education. (2016). *New Jersey state learning standards for language arts.* State of New Jersey. https://www.nj.gov/education/ standards/ela/Docs/2016NJSLS-ELA_Grade3.pdf

Derman-Sparks, L., & Ramsey, P. G. (2011). *What if all the kids are white? Anti-bias multicultural education with young children and families.* Teachers College Press.

Douglas, M. (2015, February 23). *Japanese language education of the earlier generations: From 1885 to World War II.* UCLA National Heritage Language Resource Center. https://nhlrc.ucla.edu/nhlrc/ article/150117

Duyvis, C. [@corinneduyvis]. 2015, September 6. #ownvoices, to recommend kidlit about diverse characters written by authors from that same diverse group. [Tweet]. Twitter. https://twitter.com/ corinneduyvis/status/640584099208503296?s=20&t=DlE9ys7Vgq x7POM0VZWN_A

Dyson, A. H. (2013). *ReWRITING the basics: Literacy learning in children's cultures.* Teachers College Press.

Ebarvia, T. (2019, September 5). Disrupting your texts: Why simply including diverse voices is not enough. *Literacy Now.* https://www .literacyworldwide.org/blog/literacy-now/2019/09/05/disrupting -your-texts-why-simply-including-diverse-voices-is-not-enough

Eickholdt, L., & Vitale-Reilly, P. (2022). *Writing clubs: Fostering choice, collaboration, and community in the writing classroom.* Stenhouse.

Enriquez, G. (2015). Reader response and embodied performance: Body-poems as performative response and performativity. In G. Enriquez, E. Johnson, S. Kontovourski, & C. A. Mallozzi (Eds.), *Literacies, learning, and the body: Putting theory and research into pedagogical practice.* Routledge.

Enriquez, G. (2021, July/August). Foggy mirrors, tiny windows, and heavy doors: Beyond diverse books toward meaningful literacy instruction. *The Reading Teacher, 75*(1). https://doi.org/10.1002/trtr.2030

España, C., & Herrera, L. Y. (2020). *En comunidad: Lessons for centering the voices and experiences of bilingual Latinx students.* Heinemann.

Excellent Public Schools Act of 2021, Session Law 2021-8 § 115C-83.3 *et seq.* (2021). https://lrs.sog.unc.edu/bill/excellent-public -schools-act-2021

Fairchild, H. P. (1917). The literacy test and its making. *The Quarterly Journal of Economics, 31*(3), 447–460.

Fernandes, M. I. L., Clark-Barnes, A., & Ortmeier-Hooper, C. (2022). "Units of exchange: How teachers develop assignments with academic currency for plurilingual identities. In K. M. Losey & G. Shuck (Eds.), *Plurilingual pedagogies for multilingual writing classrooms: Engaging the rich communicative repertoires of U.S. students.* Routledge.

Figueroa, M. [@megandfigueroa]. (2021, December 1). *any teacher that believes the "word gap" narrative is putting students at risk. Stop describing students as at-risk when* [Tweet]. Twitter. https://twitter .com/megandfigueroa/status/1466125567661510656?s=20&t=bKZ tQtZctjNy7iVWXHFY8w

Fisher, M. T. (2004). "The song is unfinished": The new literate and literary and their institutions. *Written Communication, 21*(3), 290–312.

Fleckenstein, K. S. (2003). *Embodied literacies: Imageword and a poetics of teaching.* Southern Illinois University Press.

Flores, N. (2018, May 31). Making millions off of the 30-million-word gap. *The Educational Linguist.* https://educationallinguist

.wordpress.com/2018/05/31/making-millions-off-of-the-30-million
-word-gap/

Flores, T. T. (2018). Breaking silence and amplifying voices: Youths writing and performing their worlds. *Journal of Adolescent & Adult Literacy, 61*(6), 653–661.

Fountas, I., & Pinnell, G. S. (2001). *Guiding readers and writers (grades 3–6): Teaching comprehension, genre, and content literacy.* Heinemann.

Fountas, I., & Pinnell, G. S. (2012a). *The F&P text level gradient revision to recommended grade-level goals.* Heinemann. https://www .heinemann.com/fountasandpinnell/pdfs/whitepapertextgrad.pdf

Fountas, I., & Pinnell, G. S. (2012b). *Fountas & Pinnell text level ladder of progress.* Heinemann. https://www.heinemann.com/ fountasandpinnell/handouts/textlevelladderofprogress.pdf

Freire, P., & Macedo, D. (1987). *Literacy: Reading the word and the world.* Bergin & Garvey.

Gabriel, M. L., Roxas, K. C., & Becker, K. (2017). Meeting, knowing, and affirming Spanish-speaking immigrant families through successful culturally responsive family engagement. *Journal of Family Diversity in Education, 2*(3), 1–18.

Gage, J. (2022). *Acquiring and using literacy.* Native American Networks. https://nativeamericannetworks.com/literacy/

Garcia, J., & Shirley, V. (2012). Performing decolonization: Lessons learned from indigenous youth, teachers and leaders' engagement with critical indigenous pedagogy. *Journal of Curriculum Theorizing, 28*(2), 76–91.

Gay, G. (2002). Preparing for culturally responsive teaching. *Journal of Teacher Education, 53*(2), 106–116.

Gay, R. (2014). *Bad feminist: Essays.* HarperCollins.

Germán, L. (2021). *Textured teaching: A framework for culturally sustaining practices.* Heinemann.

Ghiso, M. P. (2016). The laundromat as the transnational local: Young children's literacies of interdependence. *Teachers College Record, 18*(1), 1–46.

Gibson, S. (2021, November 18). *Offer of cash prize for allegations against N.H. teachers draws rebuke.* NHPR. https://www.nhpr.org/ nh-news/2021-11-18/moms-for-liberty-prize-nh-schools

Givens, J. R. (2021). *Fugitive pedagogy: Carter G. Woodson and the art of black teaching.* Harvard University Press.

Goodrich, J. M., Lonigan, C. J., & Farver, J. M. (2017). Impacts of a literacy-focused preschool curriculum on the early literacy skills of language-minority children. *Early Childhood Research Quarterly, 40*(3), 13–24.

Graff, H. J. (2010). The literacy myth: Literacy, education and demography. *Vienna Yearbook of Population Research, 8,* 17–23.

Grant, M. (1916). *The passing of the great race; or the racial basis of European history.* Charles Scribner's Sons.

Green, T. L. (2017). From positivism to critical theory: School-community relations toward community equity literacy. *International Journal of Qualitative Studies in Education, 30*(4), 370–387.

Grissom, J. A., & Redding, C. (2016). Discretion and disproportionality: Explaining the underrepresentation of high-achieving students of color in gifted programs. *AERA Open, 2*(1), 1–25.

Groeger, L. V., Waldman, A., & Eads, D. (2018, October 16). Miseducation: Is there racial inequality at your school? *ProPublica.* https://projects.propublica.org/miseducation/

Gross, J. M. S., Haines, S. J., Hill, C., Francis, G. L., Blue-Banning, M., & Turnbull, A. P. (2015). Strong school–community partnerships in inclusive schools are "part of the fabric of the school. . . . We count on them." *The School Community Journal, 25*(2), 9–34.

Gutiérrez, K., Baquedano-López, P., & Turner, M. G. (1997). Putting language back into language arts: When the radical middle meets the third space. *Language Arts, 74*(5), 368–378.

Gutiérrez, K. D. (2008). Developing sociocritical literacy in the third space. *Reading Research Quarterly, 43*(2), 148–162.

Haberman, M. (1991). The pedagogy of poverty versus good teaching. *Phi Delta Kappan, 73*(4), 290–294.

Haddix, M., & Sealey-Ruiz, Y. (2012). Cultivating digital and popular literacies as empowering and emancipatory acts among urban youth. *Journal of Adolescent & Adult Literacy, 56*(3), 189–192.

Hagood, M. C., Alvermann, D. E., & Heron-Hruby, A. (2010). *Bring it to class: Unpacking pop culture in literacy learning.* Teachers College Press.

Hall, L. A., Johnson, A. S., Juzwik, M. M., Wortham, S., & Mosley, M. (2009). Teacher identity in the context of literacy teaching: Three explorations of classroom positioning and interaction in secondary schools. *Teaching and Teacher Education, 26*(2), 234–243.

Hanford, E. (2019, January 2). *Why millions of kids can't read and what better teaching can do about it.* WBUR. https://www.wbur.org/npr/677722959/why-millions-of-kids-cant-read-and-what-better-teaching-can-do-about-it

Harper, F. E. W. (1992). Learning to read. In J. Sherman (Ed.), *African-American poetry of the nineteenth century: An anthology.* University of Illinois Press.

Harris, C. I. (1993). Whiteness as property. *Harvard Law Review, 106*(8), 1707–1791.

Harro, B. (2013). The cycle of socialization. In M. Adams, W. J. Blumenfeld, C. Castañeda, H. W. Hackman, M. L. Peters, & X. Zúñiga (Eds.), *Readings for diversity and social justice.* Routledge.

Hart, B., & Risley, T. L. (2003). The early catastrophe: The 30 million word gap by age 3. *American Educator, 27*(1), 4–9.

Hartford, B. (n.d.). *Civil rights movement voting rights: Are you "qualified" to vote? Take a "litracy test" to find out.* Civil Rights Movement Archive. https://www.crmvet.org/info/lithome.htm

Hawkins, A. (2022, March 4). *Putting your graphic novels on vacation is censorship.* Knowledge Quest. https://knowledgequest.aasl.org/putting-your-graphic-novels-on-vacation-is-censorship/

Heath, S. B. (1982). What no bedtime story means: Narrative skills at home and school. *Language in Society, 11*(1), 49–76.

Heinrich, J., Heine, S. J., & Norenzayan, A. (2010). The weirdest people in the world? *Behavioral and Brain Sciences, 33*(2/3), 1–75.

Hennessy-Fiske, M. (2022, February 3). Saving the school where kids were paddled for speaking Spanish. *Los Angeles Times.* https://www.latimes.com/world-nation/story/2022-02-03/speak-spanish-get-paddled-texas-school-segregation-mexican-americans

Holt, T. C. (1990). "Knowledge is power": The black struggle for literacy. In A. A. Lunsford, H. Moglen, and J. Slevin (Eds.), *The right to literacy.* The Modern Language Association of America.

hooks, b. (1994). *Teaching to transgress: Education as the practice of freedom*. Routledge.

H.R. 1⁵³2—112th Congress (2011–2012): Race to the Top Act of 2011. (2011, May 20). http://www.congress.gov/

Hurmence, B. (Ed.). (1994). *We lived in a little cabin in the yard*. John F. Blair.

Indians who refuse to be civilized. (1903, December 20). *The St. Paul Globe*, 38.

"Insurrection of the slaves" from the Salem Gazette. (n.d.). American Antiquarian Society. https://americanantiquarian.org/NatTurner/exhibits/show/1831reports/insurrection-of-the-slaves

Iyer, Deepa. (2018). The social change ecosystem map. *Building Movement Project*. https://buildingmovement.org/our-work/movement-building/social-change-ecosystem-map/

Janks, H. (2010). *Literacy and power*. Routledge.

Jensen, F. (2022, February 2). February, 1882: The eight box voting law severely restricts African American suffrage. *South Carolina Historical Society*. https://schistory.org/february-1882-the-eight-box-voting-law-severely-restricts-african-american-suffrage/

Johnson, G. M. (2020). *All boys aren't blue*. Farrar, Straus and Giroux.

Kaestle, C. F. (1985). The history of literacy and the history of readers. *Review of Research in Education*, *12*, 11–53. https://www.jstor.org/stable/pdf/1167145

Kamenetz, A. (2018, Ju'e 1). *Let's stop talking about the "30 million word gap."* NPR. https://www.npr.org/sections/ed/2018/06/01/615188051/lets-stop-talking-about-the-30-million-word-gap

Kee, J. C., & Carr-Chellman, D. J. (2019). Paulo Freire, critical literacy, and indigenous resistance. *Educational Studies*, *55*(1), 89–103.

Kelly, L. B., & Kachorsky, D. (2022). Text complexity and picturebooks: Learning from multimodal analysis and children's discussion. *Reading & Writing Quarterly*, *38*(1), 33–50.

Kelly, P. R., Gómez-Bellengé, F., Chen, J., & Schulz, M. M. (2008). Learner outcomes for English language learner low readers in an early intervention. *TESOL Quarterly*, *42*(2), 235–260.

Kifano, S., & Smith, E. (2003). Ebonics and education in the context of culture: Meeting the language and cultural needs of LEP African

American students. In J. Ramirez, T. Wiley, G. de Klerk, E. Lee, & W. Wright (Eds.), *Ebonics: The urban education debate*. Multilingual Matters.

Kinloch, V., Burkhard, T., & Penn, C. (2017). When school is not enough: Understanding the lives and literacies of black youth. *Research in the Teaching of English, 52*(1), 34–54.

Kirk, G., & Okazawa-Rey, M. (2013). Identities and social locations. In M. Adams, W. J. Blumenfeld, C. Castañeda, H. W. Hackman, M. L. Peters, & X. Zúñiga (Eds.), *Readings for diversity and social justice*. Routledge.

Kirkland, D. E. (2004). Rewriting school: Critical writing pedagogies for the secondary English classroom. *Journal of Teaching of Writing, 21*(1 & 2), 83–96.

Kobabe, M. (2019). *Gender queer: A memoir*. Oni Press.

Kress, G., & van Leeuwen, T. (2001). *Multimodal discourse: The modes and media of contemporary communication*. Arnold Publishers.

Ladson-Billings, G. (1995). Toward a theory of culturally relevant pedagogy. *American Educational Research Journal, 32*(3), 465–491.

Ladson-Billings, G. & Tate W. F. (1995). Toward a critical race theory of education. *Teachers College Record, 97*(1), 47–68.

Ladson-Billings, G. (2006). From the achievement gap to the education debt: Understanding achievement in U.S. schools. *Educational Researcher, 35*(7), 3–12.

Lam, W. S. E. (2006). Re-envisioning language, literacy, and the immigrant subject in new mediascapes. *Pedagogies: An International Journal, 1*(3), 171–195.

Lawrence-Lightfoot, S. (2003). *The essential conversation: What parents and teachers can learn from each other*. Random House.

Lazar, A. M., Edwards, P. A., & McMillon, G. T. (2012). *Bridging literacy and equity: The essential guide to social equity teaching*. Teachers College Press.

Lewis, J., Aydin, A., & Powell, N. (2013). *March: Book one*. Top Shelf Productions.

Li, G. (2001). Literacy as situated practice. *Canadian Journal of Education, 26*(1), 57–75.

Linan-Thompson, S. (2010). Response to instruction, English language learners and disproportionate representation: The role of assessment. *Psicothema, 22*(4), 970–974.

Love, B. J. (2013). Developing a liberatory consciousness. In M. Adams, W. J. Blumenfeld, C. Castañeda, H. W. Hackman, M. L. Peters, & X. Zúñiga (Eds.), *Readings for diversity and social justice*. Routledge.

MacPherson, K. (2020, February 27). Don't be afraid to let children read graphic novels. They're real books. *Washington Post*.

Marinkovic, K., Dhond, R. P., Dale, A. M., Glessner, M., Carr, V., & Halgren, E. (2003, May 8). Spatiotemporal dynamics of modality-specific and supramodal word processing. *Neuron, 38*(3), 487–497.

Mazariegos, M., & Sullivan, M. C. (2022, April 4). *Efforts to ban books jumped an "unprecedented" four-fold in 2021, ALA report says*. NPR. https://www.npr.org/2022/04/04/1090067026/efforts-to-ban -books-jumped-an-unprecedented-four-fold-in-2021-ala-report-says

McGhee, H. (2021). *The sum of us: What racism costs everyone and how we can prosper together*. One World.

Mehan, H. "(1979). "What time is it, Denise?": Asking known information questions in classroom discourse. *Theory Into Practice, 18*(4), 285–294.

Meltzer, E. (2020, August 7). *The misunderstanding that sparked the reading wars*. Breaking the Code: Phonics and Reading. https:// www.breakingthecode.com/the-misunderstanding-that-sparked -the-reading-wars/

Miller, S., & McVee, M. (Eds.). (2012). *Multimodal composing in classrooms*. Routledge.

Milner, H. R., IV. (2020). Disrupting racism and whiteness in researching a science of reading. *Reading Research Quarterly, 55*(S1), S249–S253.

Minor, C. (2019). *We got this: Equity, access, and the quest to be who our students need us to be*. Heinemann.

Muhammad, G. E. (2012). The literacy development and practices within African American literary societies. *Black History Bulletin, 75*(1), 6–13.

Muhammad, G. E. (2020). *Cultivating genius: An equity framework for culturally and historically responsive literacy*. Scholastic.

National Center for Education Statistics. (2021). *Racial/ethnic enrollment in public schools.* U.S. Department of Education, Institute of Education Sciences. https://nces.ed.gov/programs/coe/indicator/cge

National Commission on Excellence in Education. (1983). *A nation at risk: The imperative for educational reform: A report to the nation and the secretary of education.* National Commission on Excellence in Education.

National Federation of the Blind. (2009, March 26). *The braille literacy crisis in America: Facing the truth, reversing the trend, empowering the blind.* https://nfb.org/sites/nfb.org/files/images/nfb/documents/pdf/braille_literacy_report_web.pdf

Nelson, M. E., Hull, G. A., & Roche-Smith, J. (2008). Challenges of multimedia self-presentation: Taking, and mistaking, the show on the road. *Written Communication, 25*(4), 415–440.

New London Group. (1996). A pedagogy of multiliteracies: Designing social futures. *Harvard Educational Review, 66*(1). https://www.sfu.ca/~decaste/newlondon.htm

Newkirk, T. (2009). *Holding on to good ideas in a time of bad ones.* Heinemann.

Nixon, A. S. (2009). Mediating social thought through digital storytelling. *Pedagogies: An International Journal, 4*(1), 63–76.

No Child Left Behind Act of 2001, P.L. 107-110, 20 U.S.C. § 6319 (2002).

Nyachae, T. M. (2021). Got diverse texts? Now what? Teachers as critical guides in the moment. *Literacy Today Magazine,* (May/June), 37–39.

Nyberg, A. K. (n.d.) *Comics code history: The seal of approval.* Comic Book Legal Defense Fund. http://cbldf.org/comics-code-history-the-seal-of-approval/

Office of Special Education Programs. (2007). *27th annual (2005) report to Congress on the implementation of the Individuals with Disabilities Education Act* (Vol. 1). U.S. Department of Education. https://files.eric.ed.gov/fulltext/ED499021.pdf

Okun, T. (1999). *White supremacy culture.* White Supremacy Culture. https://www.whitesupremacyculture.info/uploads/4/3/5/7/43579015/okun_-_white_sup_culture_2020.pdf

Okun, T. (n.d.). *Worship of the written word.* White Supremacy Culture.

Retrieved May 22, 2022, from https://www.whitesupremacyculture .info/worship-of-written-word.html

Ortmeier-Hooper, C. (2013). *The ELL writer: Moving beyond basics in the secondary classroom.* Teachers College Press.

Orton, S. T. (1929). The "sight reading" method of teaching reading, as a source of reading disability. *Journal of Educational Psychology, 20*(2), 135–143.

Owocki, G., & Goodman, Y. (2002). *Kidwatching: Documenting children's literacy development.* Heinemann.

Pacheko, M. B., & Smith, B. E. (2015). Across languages, modes, and identities: Bilingual adolescents' multimodal codemeshing in the literacy classroom. *Bilingual Research Journal, 38*(3), 292–312.

Pahl, K. (2011). My family, my story: Exploring time and space through digital storytelling projects. In S. S. Abrams and J. Rowsell (Eds.), *Rethinking identity and literacy education in the 21st century.* Teachers College Press.

Palmeri, J. (2012). *Remixing composition: A history of multimodal writing pedagogy.* Southern Illinois University Press.

Parker, K. N. (2022). *Literacy is liberation: Working toward justice through culturally relevant teaching.* ASCD.

Placier, M. (1996). The cycle of student labels in education: The cases of culturally deprived disadvantaged and at risk. *Educational Administration Quarterly, 32*(2), 236–270.

Polo, M. J. (2022, June 2). *Michigan prisons ban Spanish and Swahili dictionaries to prevent inmate disruptions.* NPR. https://www.npr .org/2022/06/02/1102164439/michigan-prisons-ban-spanish-and -swahili-dictionaries-to-prevent-inmate-disrupti

Postman, N., & Weingartner, C. (1969). *Teaching as a subversive activity.* Dell Publishing.

Pounder, C. C. H., Adelman, L., Cheng, J., Herbes-Sommers, C., Strain, T. H., Smith, L., & Ragazzi, C. (2003). *Race: The power of an illusion* [Film]. California Newsreel.

Pranikoff, K. (2017). *Teaching talk: A practical guide to fostering student thinking and conversation.* Heinemann.

Prendergast, C. (2003). *Literacy and social justice: The politics of learning after* Brown v. Board of Education. Southern Illinois University Press.

Price, M. (2019, November 17). Menace lurked between pages. *Akron Beacon Journal.* https://www.beaconjournal.com/story/lifestyle/around-town/2019/11/17/menace-lurked-between-pages/2269493007/

Price-Dennis, D. (2016). Developing curriculum to support black girls' literacies in digital spaces. *English Education, 48*(4), 337–361.

Price-Dennis, D., Muhammad, G. E., Womack, E., McArthur, S. A., & Haddix, M. (2017). The multiple identities and literacies of black girlhood: A conversation about creating spaces for black girl voices. *Journal of Language & Literacy Education, 13*(2), 1–18.

Purcell-Gates, V., Jacobson, E., & Degener, S. (2004). *Print literacy development: Uniting cognitive and social practice theories.* Harvard University Press.

Pyle, K. C., & Cunningham, S. (2014). *Bad for you: Exposing the war on fun!* Henry Holt.

Reynolds, J. (2020). The ingredients. In I. Zoboi (Ed.), *Black enough: Stories of being young and black in America.* HarperCollins.

Rochester, M. J. (2002). *Class warfare: Besieged schools, bewildered parents, betrayed kids and the attack on excellence.* Encounter Books.

Rogoff, B., Dahl, A., & Callanan, M. A. (2018). The importance of understanding children's lived experience. *Developmental Review, 50*(A), 5–15.

Rosa, J., & Flores, N. (2017). Do you hear what I hear? Raciolinguistic ideologies and culturally sustaining pedagogies. In D. Paris & H. S. Alim (Eds.), *Culturally sustaining pedagogies: Teaching and learning for justice in a changing world.* Teachers College Press.

Rosenblatt, L. (1978). *The reader, the text, the poem: The transactional theory of the literary work.* Southern Illinois University Press.

Ruiz, V. L. (2001). South by southwest: Mexican Americans and segregated schooling, 1900–1950. *OAH Magazine of History, 15*(2), 23–27.

Runton, A. (2004). *Owly: Vol. 1. The way home and the bittersweet summer.* Top Shelf Productions.

Safir, S., & Dugan, J. (2021). *Street data: A next-generation model for equity, pedagogy, and school transformation.* Corwin.

Satrapi, M. (2003). *Persepolis: The story of a childhood.* Pantheon.

Scarborough, H. S. (2001). Connecting early language and literacy to later reading (dis)abilities: Evidence, theory, and practice. In S. Neuman & D. Dickinson (Eds.), *Handbook for research in early literacy* (pp. 97–110). Guilford Press.

Scheel, N. P., & Branch, R. C. (1993). The role of conversation and culture in the systematic design of instruction. *Educational Technology*, *33*(8), 7–18.

Schwartz, R. G. (1997). Why Johnny 's parents can't read . . . or vote, or work, or participate: The national literacy crisis and a proposal to integrate illiterate adults into mainstream American society. *The University of Chicago Law School Roundtable*, *4*(1), 183–230.

Scoggin, J., & Schneewind, H. (2021). *Trusting readers: Powerful practices for independent reading.* Heinemann.

Scribner, C. F. (2020). Surveying the destruction of African American schoolhouses in the South, 1864–1876. *Journal of the Civil War Era*, *10*(4), 469–494.

Share, D. L. (2021). Is the science of reading just the science of reading English? *Reading Research Quarterly*, *56*(S1), S391–S402.

Sheffield, R. M., D'Andrea, F. M., Morash, V., & Chatfield, S. (2022). How many braille readers? Policy, politics, and perception. *Journal of Visual Impairment and Blindness*, *166*(1), 14–25.

Silverman, A. M., & Bell, E. C. (2018). The association between braille reading history and well-being for blind adults. *Journal of Blindness Innovation and Research*, *8*(1). https://nfb.org/images/nfb/publications/jbir/jbir18/jbir080103.html

Smith, B. E., Pacheco, M. B., & de Almeida, C. R. (2017). Multimodal codemeshing: Bilingual adolescents' processes composing across modes and languages. *Journal of Second Language Writing, 36*, 6–22.

Smith, J. M., & Pole, K. (2018). What's going on in a graphic novel? *The Reading Teacher*, *72*(2), 169–177.

Smith, L. T. (2008). *Decolonizing methodologies: Research and indigenous peoples.* University of Otago Press.

Soontornvat, C. (2020). *A wish in the dark.* Candlewick.

Span, C. M. (2005). Learning in spite of opposition: African Americans and their history of educational exclusion in antebellum America. *Counterpoints*, *131*, 26–53.

Sperry, D. E., Sperry, L. L., & Miller, P. J. (2019). Reexamining the verbal environments of children from different socioeconomic backgrounds. *Child Development*, *90*(4), 1303–1318.

Spivak, G. C. (1992). Teaching for the times. *The Journal of the Midwest Modern Language Association*, *25*(1), 3–22.

Stefanski, A., Valli, L., & Jacobson, R. (2016). Beyond involvement and engagement: The role of the family in school–community partnerships. *School Community Journal*, *26*(2), 135–160.

Stewart, L. (2020). *The science of reading: Evidence for a new era of reading instruction*. Zaner-Bloser. https://www.zaner-bloser.com/reading/superkids-reading-program/pdfs/Whitepaper_TheScienceofReading.pdf

Stivers, J. (2015, April 28). Native American representation in children's literature: Challenging the "people of the past" narrative. *American Indians in Children's Literature*. https://americanindiansinchildrensliterature.blogspot.com/2015/04/native-american-representation-in.html

Stockman, A. (2021). *Creating inclusive writing environments in the K–12 classroom: Reluctance, resistance, and strategies that make a difference*. Routledge.

Street, B. (1984). *Literacy in theory and practice*. Cambridge University Press.

Street, B. (2001). The new literacy studies. In E. Cushman, G. R. Kintgen, B. M. Kroll, & M. Rose (Eds.), *Literacy: A critical sourcebook* (pp. 430–442). St. Martin's Press.

Street, B. (2011). Literacy inequalities in theory and practice: The power to name and define. *International Journal of Educational Development*, *31*(6), 580–586.

Stringfellow, L. (2019, May 10). Teaching and writing in the intersection. *#31DaysIBPOC*. http://www.lstringfellow.com/blog/31daysibpoc-teaching-and-writing-in-the-intersection

Stuckey, J. E. (1991). *The violence of literacy*. Heinemann.

Talusan, L. A. (2022). *The identity-conscious educator: Building habits and skills for a more inclusive school*. Solution Tree Press.

Tatum, B. D. (2013). The complexity of identity: Who am I? In M. Adams, W. J. Blumenfeld, C. Castañeda, H. W. Hackman, M. L.

Peters, & X. Zúñiga (Eds.), *Readings for diversity and social justice*. Routledge.

TEDx. (2016, March 18). *Grace Lin: The windows and mirrors of your child's bookshelf* [Video]. YouTube. https://www.youtube.com/watch?v=_wQ8wiV3FVo

Tilly, C. (1998). Changing forms of inequality. *Sociological Theory*, *21*(1), 31–36.

Trimbur, J. (1991). Literacy and the discourse of crisis. In R. Bullock & J. Trimbur (Eds.), *The Politics of writing instruction: Postsecondary* (pp. 277–295). Boynton/Cook Publishers.

Tyson, K. (2011). *Integration interrupted: Tracking, black students, and acting white after Brown*. Oxford University Press.

University of Oregon (2021). *8th edition of Dynamic Indicators of Basic Early Literacy Skills (DIBELS)*. https://dibels.uoregon.edu/

Valencia, S. W. (2010). Authentic classroom assessment of early reading: Alternatives to standardized tests. *Preventing School Failure: Alternative Education for Children and Youth*, *41*(2), 63–70.

Varnum, R. (1986). From crisis to crisis: The evolution toward higher standards of literacy in the united states. *Rhetoric Society Quarterly*, *16*(3), 145–165.

Vetter, A. (2010). Positioning students as readers and writers through talk in a high school English classroom. *English Education*, *43*(1), 33–64.

Vogrinčič, A. (2008). The novel-reading panic in 18th-century in England: An outline of an early moral media panic. *Medijska Istraživanja*, *14*(2), 103–124.

Voss, K. (2010). Enduring legacy? Charles Tilly and durable inequality. *The American Sociologist, (41)*, 368–374.

Votruba-Drzal, E., Li-Grining, C. P., & Maldonado-Carreño, C. (2008). A developmental perspective on full- versus part-day kindergarten and children's academic trajectories through fifth grade. *Child Development*, *79*(4), 957–978.

Wan, A. J. (2014). *Producing good citizens: Literacy training in anxious times*. University of Pittsburgh Press.

Weil, J. Z. (2019, April 30). The Bible was used to justify slavery. Then Africans made it their path to freedom. *Washington Post*. https://www

.washingtonpost.com/local/the-bible-was-used-to-justify-slavery
-then-africans-made-it-their-path-to-freedom/2019/04/29/34699e8e
-6512-11e9-82ba-fcfeff232e8f_story.html

Wexler, N. (2022, May 29). Here's what states can do to truly boost student literacy. *Minding the Gap.* https://nataliewexler.substack.com/p/heres-what-states-can-do-to-truly?s=w

Wiggins, G. P. (1993). *Assessing student performance: Exploring the purpose and limits of testing.* Jossey-Bass.

Will, M. (2020, April 14). *Still mostly white and female: New federal data on the teaching profession.* Education Week. https://www.edweek.org/leadership/still-mostly-white-and-female-new-federal-data-on-the-teaching-profession/2020/04

Williams, H. A. (2007). *Self-taught: African American education in slavery and freedom.* University of North Carolina Press.

Winn, M. T., & Behizadeh, N. (2011). The right to be literate: Literacy, education, and the school-to-prison pipeline. *Review of Research in Education, 35,* 147–173.

Winn, M. T. (2015). Exploring the literate trajectories of youth across time and space. *Mind, Culture, and Activity, 22*(1), 58–67.

Woodson, C. G. (1919). *The education of the Negro prior to 1861.* The Associated Publishers.

Woodson, J. (2018, February 5). *Stop using the label "struggling reader," author Jacqueline Woodson advises.* Education Week. https://www.edweek.org/teaching-learning/stop-using-the-label-struggling-reader-author-jacqueline-woodson-advises/2018/02

Yang, K. (2019). *How do you deal with being teased at school?* [Video]. Front Desk: The Book. https://frontdeskthebook.com/for-teachers/